# MINDFULNESS AT WORK

A PRACTICAL GUIDE TO

ENHANCE YOUR FOCUS AND ATTENTION, ACHIEVE BETTER RESULTS (DOING LESS!) AND IMPROVE YOUR WELL-BEING

**NIEVES RODRÍGUEZ**

First published in UK in 2020 by Nieves Rodriguez
This First Edition in English published in 2020 by
Nieves Rodríguez

**Copyright © 2020 by Nieves Rodríguez**

Fastracktorefocus is a Trademark

All rights reserved.
No part of this publication may be reproduced, stored in a retrieval system, or transmitted, in any form or by any means, without the prior permission in writing of the publisher, nor be otherwise circulated in any form of binding or cover than that which it is published and without a similar condition including this condition being imposed on the subsequent purchaser.

**ISBN:** 9798573368108

**Printed in UK**

www. fastracktorefocus.com

*This book is dedicated to the most
important people in my life: Khali, Noelia
and Zidane and to my wonderful family,
especially to my Mum who through her
experience taught me to be strong,
free and enjoy every minute of my life.*

*I love you all more than I can put into words.*

*And to you, the reader, for being here. If you are reading these words, you are making this world a better place.*

Change lives with your actions.

## MISSION

This year has been specially challenging for many people. On a personal and professional dimension.

There is no doubt that the times of crisis, turmoil and great change are here only to stay and increase. Many people suffer from uncertainty and insecurity. People start asking questions that they thought they would never have to, and the most useful answers will be the ones that emerge from within each of us. We may not be able to stabilize the economy, but we can find personal stability within economic instability.

You can't avoid turbulences. You can only navigate through them and this is why Mindfulness, -awareness, focus and attention-is a vital skill for any person.

We are all leaders. Leaders of our life.

Companies are made of individuals, leaders with and without a title. Organizations do not change, people do…or they don't…

Leaders for the future need to have values and vision and to be authentic and agile, aligned and on purpose. Add awareness and responsibility to the mix, self-belief and a good measure of emotional intelligence and we have a powerful recipe.

(VVAAAP)+ (AR)+ Self+EQ = leaders

Whether you have a leadership title in your busines card or not, you are a leader of your life.

Be the change you want to see in your organisation and in your life.

Mindful people> Mindful Employees>Mindful Leaders> Mindful Organisations>Mindful World

Thank you for allowing me to be part of this change. Our journey together is about to begin.

With love and gratitude,

*Nieves*

# CONTENTS

| | |
|---|---|
| **MISSION** | 7 |
| **CONTENTS** | 9 |
| **MINDFULNESS AT WORK** | 11 |
| | |
| **WHAT IS HAPPENING** | 15 |
| ARE YOU HUMAN BEING OR HUMAN DOING? | 19 |
| OUR BUSY MINDS | 25 |
| CREATE MENTAL SPACE | 35 |
| CHANGE | 39 |
| AUTOPILOT | 45 |
| | |
| **COLLABORATING WITH YOUR MIND** | 49 |
| ACTION ADDICTION | 51 |
| COLLABORATING WITH YOUR MIND | 55 |
| WORK AS AN ADULT, OBSERVE AS A ACHILD | 67 |
| MINDFULNESS AND ITS BENEFITS | 71 |
| LET´S GO TO THE GYM | 79 |
| NAM-TOK | 81 |
| THE PRESENT | 83 |
| AWARENESS AND LASER FOCUS | 87 |
| | |
| **WORK TECHNIQUES** | 95 |
| WHY DO WE NEED MINDFULNESS AT WORK? | 97 |
| YOUR AREA OF CONTROL | 99 |
| MINDFUL E-MAILS | 103 |
| MINDFUL MEETINGS | 115 |
| MINDFUL GOALS | 119 |
| MINDFUL PRIORITIES | 125 |
| MINDFUL PLANNING | 131 |
| MINDFUL COMMUNICATION | 137 |
| MINDFUL CREATIVITY | 141 |
| MINDFUL COMMUTING | 145 |
| MINDFUL BREAKS | 149 |
| | |
| **WELL BEING** | 153 |
| CONSERVE YOUR ENERGY | 155 |
| MINDFUL EXERCISE | 157 |

| | |
|---|---|
| EATING MINDFULLY | 161 |
| ENJOYING SLEEP | 165 |
| | |
| **THE HOLISTIC YOU** | 177 |
| HOLISTIC APPROACH TO LIFE | 179 |
| EMOTIONAL BALANCE | 185 |
| KINDNESS | 189 |
| CULTIVATE JOY | 195 |
| | |
| **MINDFULNESS AT WORKPLACE** | 201 |
| MINDFUL LEADERS | 203 |
| INTRODUCING MINDFULNESS AT THE WORKPLACE | 208 |
| | |
| **LIFE IS A STORY** | 211 |
| | |
| **ANNEX** | 213 |
| MINDFULNESS AT WORK PROGRAM | 215 |
| BREATHING | 217 |
| | |
| **SERVICES AVAILABLE** | 221 |
| | |
| **ABOUT THE AUTHOR** | 223 |

> Mindfulness is the new smartphone.
> you can use it anywhere, in anyplace,
> in any areas of your life
>
> -Nieves

# Mindfulness At Work

To be honest, I am probably the last person one might expect to write about mindfulness, as I have always been considered a busy bee, but years ago, I had a series of profound insights and realizations that changed my perspective in a significant way.

First, I realized my brain was full—full of all of the things associated with living a high-pressure, fast-paced, demanding life. Second, I realized that I essentially had assumed that having a "full brain" was unavoidable and that if I wanted to be a successful leader in one of the world's largest airlines, it was simply part of the "package."

However, I discovered another way of working and being that not only freed up brain capacity but also made me more effective, more creative, less stressed, and most probably more kind. These realizations have inspired me to study and practice Mindfulness, Executive Coaching and NLP.

In today's "always-on" technology, constant data over-load, and extreme time pressure to the work that we do, even the best, brightest, most mentally strong, and talented people are sometimes unable to cope. Stress can be a debilitating illness, and the constant pressure of working in a corporate world drove me to search for tools for enhancing sustainable performance, tools that could help my people and me do the work we love, while performing at the highest level, but without sacrificing well-being and balance in life.

I felt I needed this ME time and since I focused my attention to personal development, I felt I was happier and a better person at home and at work.

Years ago, I decided to do my Master in Corporate & Executive Coaching and most recently I became NLP and Mindfulness Practitioner and Master. They have made a huge difference in my work, leadership, and private life, well as for the people on my team. I am convinced it can do the same for you.

Work life has changed radically over the past few decades. People used to be able to focus their full attention on each and every task. Now they attempt to concentrate on work while dealing with a constant stream of text messages, e-mails, phone calls, meetings, and deadlines. Faced with a relentless flood of information and distractions, our brains try to process everything at once. In other words, we try to multitask.

But researchers have shown that multitasking is the worst possible reaction to information overload. According to a McKinsey &Company report, multitasking actually "makes human beings less productive, less creative, and less able to make good decisions." In fact, numerous studies have found that modern office life is transforming competent professionals into frenzied underachievers.

Are we destined to have minds that constantly wander, remain inattentive, and lose focus?

Thankfully, the answer is no. It is actually possible to train the brain to respond differently to today's constant interruptions through the practice of mindfulness.

Simply put, at its introductory level, mindfulness means trained attention. Based on thousands of years of practice, mindfulness techniques enable people to manage their attention, improve their awareness, and sharpen their focus and clarity.

The key is to have a holistic view of your life and applying mindfulness techniques to daily work & life.

I have created a program to bring in corporate mindfulness providing real-world techniques that you can implement and get increases in productivity, effectiveness, job satisfaction, and much more. The quantitative results of this program include increased focus and effectiveness, as well as enhanced quality of life, reduced stress, and better well-being.

On an individual level, the program has helped people quickly and easily learn how to improve efficiency and increase self-control.

"Speed wins," we often say. As human beings, we want information now; we want to take action in the moment. Whenever we are given a choice, we will opt for a service that delivers faster than the competition.

And from a cognitive perspective, being ahead provides a clear edge in effectiveness and productivity. It offers the space and freedom to choose your distractions and direct your mental energy

In the end, this is what mindfulness is. Mindfulness is about being our best selves and realizing more of our potential in everyday life. People who are more focused, clear minded, and kind make for better organizations. And many better organizations make for a better world. Think of a world in which improving performance goes hand in hand with increasing kindness. And a world in which kindness is valued as much as efficiency and effectiveness, as much as revenue per share or operating cash flow.

It may sound overly optimistic, but I see it happening every day in the many organizations we serve around the globe.

Designed for busy professionals looking for a new way of working within high-stress, high-paced conditions, this book has been written as a very practical, how-to guide that you , your team, your family can implement from day one. If you wish to, you can introduce these techniques gradually by following my 8 weeks -Mindfulness At Work Program - (see Appendix)

Though the techniques will be of great interest to individuals in leadership roles, it has been developed to be highly relevant and applicable for people at all levels of an organization. Offering small, bite-sized techniques, the system tackles the most persistent inefficiencies and problems in the workday, such as e-mail, meetings, priorities, and planning. Each of these techniques is self-contained and easily implemented, providing readers with immediate results.

This book and my Mindfulness At Work Program aim to change that by starting where busy people like you—need immediate assistance: with the daily tasks that sap energy and reduce productivity. Once you have experienced success with these tasks, you can explore deeper mindfulness interventions that address the development of mental qualities such as presence, patience, kindness, and acceptance. From there, it is an easy step to transforming your life through the regular practice of mindfulness and its core tenets: sharp focus and open awareness.

In the following pages I will share:

- Tools and techniques for implementing mindfulness at work to enhance focus, clarity, and results
- Tools to mindfully manage emails, meetings, goal setting, priorities…and many more
- Habits that you can introduce each week to increase mindfulness in all areas of your life
- Mindful habits to improve your well being
- Tips to introduce Mindfulness in your life and business
- In each chapter you have a Mindfulness At Work- Quick Start tips
- And should you choose to accept the challenge, I am sharing with you an 8 weeks downloadable Mindfulness At Work Program to accompany you during this journey. See Appendix.

And for ease, the book has been divided into different sections to help you introduce mindfulness at work and navigate through it – and revisit-as you need it more:

- What is Happening
- What is Mindfulness and its Benefits
- Collaborating with your Mind
- Work Strategies
- Well-Being Tips
- The Holistic You
- How to Introduce Mindfulness in your Life and in your Organisation
- Annex- 8 weeks Mindfulness At Work Program

This program is inspired by the hundreds of people that I have worked with and in my personal journey.

I hope it will be of long-lasting benefit to you. By practicing the methods only a few minutes a day, you can develop more effective mental habits, allowing you to thrive in even the most competitive, high-pressure situations. Most important, however, these techniques are intended to empower you— and busy people like you—by providing a road map to improving performance through greater focus, awareness and clarity of mind and conscious leadership.

Conscious Leadership in all areas of your life. Because you are the leader of your own life.

All the best

*Nieves*

# WHAT IS HAPPENING?

The present moment is the only time over which we have dominion.

Thích Nhất Hạnh

## Are you a human being or a human doing?

Viewing your life from a different place can equally transform your feelings. Think back to a time when you were getting ready for a well-earned holiday. There was far too much to do and simply not enough time to cram it all in. You got home late from work after trying and failing to 'clear the decks' before allowing yourself to take time off. You felt like a hamster trapped in a wheel going round and round and round. Even deciding what to take with you was fraught with difficulties. By the time the packing was complete, you felt exhausted and then had trouble sleeping because your mind was still churning through all of the things you'd been working on throughout the day. In the morning, you woke up, put all the bags in the locked the house up and drove away. And that was it.

A short while later you were lying on a beautiful beach, laughing, and joking with your friends. Work and its priorities were suddenly a million miles away and you could hardly remember them at all. You felt refreshed and whole again because your entire world had shifted gear. Your work still existed, of course, but you were seeing it from a different place. Nothing more.

Time can also fundamentally alter your outlook on life. Think back to the last time you had an argument with a colleague or a stranger perhaps with someone in a call centre? The after-effects of the argument probably ruined your whole day. Yet a few weeks later the event still happened, but you were remembering it from a different point in time. Nothing more.

Changing your perspective can transform your experience of life, as the above examples show. But they also expose a fundamental problem -they all occurred because something outside of you had changed: the sun came out, you went on holiday, time passed. And, the trouble is, if you rely solely on outside circumstances changing in order to feel happy and energised, you'll have to wait a very long time. And while you wait, constantly hoping that the sun will come out or wishing that could travel to the peace and tranquillity of an imagined future or an idealised past, your actual life will slip by unnoticed. Those moments might as well not exist at all.

**But it doesn't have to be this way.**

Negative feelings persist when the mind's problem-solving Doing mode volunteers to help, but instead ends up compounding the very difficulties you were seeking to overcome.

But there is an alternative. Our minds also have a different way of relating to the world. It's called the 'Being mode'. It's similar but far more than a shift in perspective. It's a different way of knowing that allows you to see how your mind tends to distort 'reality'. It helps you to step outside of your mind's natural tendency to over-think, over-analyse and over-judge. You begin to experience the world directly, so you can see any distress you're feeling from a totally new angle and handle life's difficulties very differently. And you find that you can change your internal landscape (the mindscape if you will) irrespective of what's happening around you. You are no longer dependent on external circumstances for your happiness. You are back in control of your life.

**If Doing mode is a trap, then Being mode is freedom**.

Mindfulness is the door through which you can enter this 'Being 'mode and, with a little practice, you can learn to open this door whenever you need to.

In mindfulness, we start to see the world as it is not as we expect it to be, how we want it to be, or what we fear it might become.

These ideas may initially seem a little too nebulous to grasp fully. By their very nature they have to be experienced to be properly understood. So, to ease this process along, the structure of this book is to start putting things into practice so you can feel and experience the benefits.

Remember than the doing mode is not an enemy to be defeated but is often an ally. Doing mode only becomes a 'problem' when its volunteers for a task that it cannot do, such as 'solving' a troubling emotion. When this happens, it pays to 'shift gear' into 'being mode'.

This is what mindfulness gives us: the ability to shift gears as we need to, rather than being permanently stuck in the same one.

Mindfulness acts like a gentle alarm bell that tells you, for example, when you are over-thinking and reminds you that there is an alternative: that you still have choices, no matter how unhappy, stressed, or frantic you might feel.

We must stress again that mindful acceptance is not resignation. Mindfulness is a 'coming to your senses'. It gives you a tremendous sense of perspective. You can sense what is important and what is not.

***Mindfulness and Resilience***

Mindfulness has been found to boost resilience – that is, the ability to withstand life's knocks and setbacks to quite a remarkable degree. Hardiness varies hugely from person to person. Some people thrive on stressful challenges that may daunt many others, whether these involve meeting ever-increasing work performance targets, trekking to the South Pole or being able to cope with three kids, a stressful job and mortgage payments.

What is it that makes 'hardy' people able to cope where others might wilt? Dr Suzanne Kobasa at City University of New York narrowed the field down to three psychological traits which she termed control, commitment, and challenge.

So 'hardy' people have a belief that their situation has inherent meaning that they can commit themselves to, that they can manage their life and that their situation is understandable that it is basically comprehensible, even if it seems chaotic and out of control.

But perhaps most intriguing of all is the realisation that these "fundamental character" traits are not unchangeable after all.

They can be changed for the better by just eight weeks of mindfulness practice. And these transformations should not be underestimated because they can have huge significance for our day-to-day lives. While empathy, compassion and inner serenity are vital for overall wellbeing, a certain degree of hardiness is required too. And the cultivation of mindfulness can have a dramatic impact on these crucial aspects of our lives.

The things that matter most in our lives are not fantastic or grand. They are moments when we touch one another.

Jack Kornfield

## Our Busy Minds

We all go through life with rises and falls in mood and energy. Often these changes in mood come out of the blue. One moment we're happily bumbling through life, daydreaming, feeling content and unfussed, but then something subtle happens. Before we know it, we're starting to feel a little stressed: there is too much to do and not enough time, and the pace of demands seems ever-more relentless. We feel tired but find that even after a good night's sleep we don't feel refreshed. And then we stop and ask ourselves: How did that happen? There may have been no big changes in life, we haven't lost any friends nor have our debts suddenly spiralled out of control. Nothing's changed, but the joy has somehow gone out of life and been replaced with a sort of generalised distress and listlessness.

Most people, most of the time, do scape out of these downward spirals. Such periods do generally pass. But sometimes they can tip us into a tailspin that persists for days. Or, sometimes, they can persist for weeks and months with no apparent rhyme or reason. In severe cases, people can be tipped into a full-blown episode of clinical anxiety or depression.

***Unhappiness, stress, and depression***

Depression is taking a staggering toll on the modern world. Around 10 per cent of the population can expect to become clinically depressed over the coming year. And things are likely to become worse. The World Health Organization estimates that depression will impose the second-biggest health burden globally by 2020. Think about that for a moment. Depression will impose a bigger burden than heart disease, arthritis, and many forms of cancer on both individuals and society in less than a decade.

Depression used to be an illness of the late middle-aged; now it strikes most people first when they are in their mid-twenties, and a substantial number of people suffer their first around their teens. It can also persist, with around 15-39 per cent of sufferers stills depressed after one year. Around one-fifth remain depressed for two or more years -the definition of chronic depression. But the scariest thing of all is that depression tends to return. If you have been depressed once, there is a 50 % per cent chance of recurrence-even if you have made a full recovery.

Depression may be exacting a staggering toll but its cousin chronic anxiety- is becoming disturbingly common too, with average levels of anxiety in children and young people now at a point that would have been judged to be "clinical' in the 1950s.It's not a great stretch of the imagination to assume that in a few decades unhappiness, depression and anxiety will have become the normal human condition, rather than happiness and contentment.

Although persistent periods of distress and exhaustion often seem to arrive from nowhere, there are underlying processes going on in the background of the mind that were only unravelled in the 1990s and early twenty-first century. And with this understanding has come the realisation that we can 'step outside' of our troubles and liberate ourselves from unhappiness, anxiety, stress, exhaustion and even depression.

**Our troubled minds**

Emotions are like a background colour that's created when your mind fuses together all of your thoughts, feelings, impulses and bodily sensations to conjure up an overall guiding theme or state of mind. All of these different elements that make up an emotion play off each other and can end up enhancing overall mood.

Several decades ago, it became apparent that thoughts could drive our moods and emotions, but it's only since the 1980s that it's become clear that the process can also run in reverse: moods can drive our thoughts. Think about that for a moment. Your moods can drive your thoughts. In practice, this means that even a few fleeting moments of sadness can end up feeding off themselves to create more unhappy thoughts by colouring how you see and interpret the world. Just as gloomy skies can make you feel, well, gloomy, momentary sadness can dredge up unsettling thoughts and memories further deepening the mood. The same goes for other moods and emotions too. If you feel stressed, then this stress can feed off itself to create more stress. Likewise, with anxiety, fear, anger, and such 'positive' emotions as love, happiness, compassion, and empathy.

But it is not just thoughts and moods that feed off each other and end up wreaking wellbeing-the body also gets involved. This is because the mind does not exist in isolation; it's a fundamental part of the body and they both continuously share emotional information with each other. In fact, much of what the body feels is coloured by our thought and emotions, and everything that we think is informed by what's going on in the body. It is a phenomenally complex process full of feedbacks, but research is showing us that our whole outlook on life can be shifted by tiny changes in the body. Something as simple as smiling or altering a posture can have a dramatic impact on mood and the types of thoughts flickering across the mind.

To get a flavour of how powerful this feedback can be, the psychologists Fritz Strack, Leonard Martin and Sabine Stepperó asked a group of people to watch cartoons and then rate how funny they were. Some were asked to hold a pencil between their lips so that they were forced to purse them and mimic their teeth, simulating a smile. The results were striking who were forced to smile found the cartoons significantly funnier than those compelled to frown. It's obvious that smiling show you are happy, but it is, a bit strange to realise that the act of smiling can itself make you happy. It's a perfect illustration of just how close the links are between the mind and body. Smiling is infectious too. When one grin, you almost invariably smile back. You can't help it.

Think about that for a moment: just the act of smiling can make you happy (even if it's forced); and if you smile, others will smile back at you, reinforcing your own happiness. It's a virtuous cycle.

But there's an equal and opposite vicious cycle too: when we sense a threat we tense up, ready to fight or run away. This so called "fight-or-flight response isn't conscious – it's controlled by one of the most 'primeval parts of the brain, which means it's often a bit simplistic in the way it interprets danger. In fact, it makes no distinction between an external threat, such as a tiger, and an internal one, such as a troubling memory or a future worry. It treats both as threats that either need to be fought off or run away from. When a threat is sensed whether real or imagined - the body tenses and braces for action. You feel tension in the shoulders or the draining of blood from the skin. The mind then senses the tension in the body and interprets it as a threat which then makes the body tense up even further...A vicious cycle has begun.

In practice, this means that if you're feeling a little stressed or vulnerable, a minor emotional shift can end up ruining your whole day - or even tip you into a prolonged period of dissatisfaction or worry. Such shifts often appear out of the blue, leaving you drained of energy and asking, why am I so unhappy?

Gradually, the repeated triggering of negative thoughts and moods can begin wearing grooves in the mind; over time, these become deeper and deeper, making it easier to set off negative, self-critical thoughts and low or panicky moods – and more difficult to shake them off. After a while, prolonged periods of fragility can be triggered by the most innocuous of things, such a momentary dipping mood or at the slightest flux in energy levers. These triggers can be so small that you might not even be aware of them.

The close links between the different aspects of emotion, stretching back into the past, can explain why a small trigger can have a significant effect on mood. Sometimes these moods come and go just as quickly as they arrive, but sometimes, the stress and fatigue, or the low mood, seen adhesive-they stick around, and nothing seems to get rid of them. It is almost like certain parts of the mind switch on, then get stuck and refuse to turn off again. As it turns out, this is what seen to be happening: sometimes the mind automatically switches to full alert, but then does not switch off again, as it's meant to do.

A good way of illustrating this is to observe the ways in which many animals deal with danger as compared to humans. Cast your mind back to the last nature documentary you saw on TV. Perhaps it contained scenes of a herd of gazelles being chased by a leopard on the African savannah. Terrified, the animals ran like crazy until the leopard had either caught one or gave up the chase for the day. Once the danger had passed, the herd quickly settled the gave back into grazing. Something in the gazelles' brains that alarm when the leopard was noticed, switched off once the danger was past.

But the human mind is different, especially when it comes to the 'intangible threats' that can trigger anxiety, stress, worry or irritability. When there is something to be scared or stressed about whether real or imagined our ancient 'fight-or-flight reactions kick in as they should. But then something else happens: the mind begins to look through memories to try and find something that will explain why we are feeling like this.

So, if we feel stressed or in danger, our minds dig up memories of when we felt threatened in the past, and then create scenarios of what might happen in the future if we cannot explain what is going on now. The result is that the brain's alarm signals start to be triggered not only by the current scare, but by past threats and future worries. This happens in an instant, before we're even aware of it.

This is why in mindfulness is so important to label our feelings. Unlike the gazelles, we don't stop running.

And this holds true for our human feelings and emotions including unhappiness, anxiety, and stress. When we're unhappy, for example, it's natural to try and figure out why we're feeling this way and to find a way of solving the problem of unhappiness. But tension, unhappiness or exhaustion aren't 'problems' that can be solved. They are emotions. They reflect states of mind and body. As such, they cannot be solved only felt. Once you've felt them that is, acknowledged their existence and let go of the tendency to explain or get rid of them, they are much more likely to vanish naturally, like the mist on a spring morning.

Why do your best efforts to get rid of unpleasant feelings backfire so tragically?

When you try and solve the problem' of unhappiness (or any other 'negative emotion) you deploy one of the mind's most powerful tools: rational critical thinking. It works like this: you see yourself in a place (unhappy) and know where you want to be (happy). Your mind then analyses the gap between the two and tries to work out the best way of bridging it. To do so it uses its 'Doing' mode (so called because it performs well in solving problems and getting things done). The 'Doing' mode works by progressively narrowing the gap between where you are and where you want to be. It does so by subconsciously breaking down the problem into pieces, each of which is solved in your mind's eye and the solution re-analysed to see whether it's got closer to your goal. It often happens in an instant and we're you frequently not even aware of the process. It's a tremendously powerful way of solving problems. It's how we find our way across cities, drive cars and arrange hectic work schedules

It's perfectly natural, then, to apply this approach to solving the "problem" of unhappiness. But it's often the worst thing you can do because it requires you to focus on the gap between how you are and how you'd like to be: in doing so, you ask such critical questions as, What's wrong with me? Where did I go wrong? Such questions are not only harsh and self-destructive, but they also demand that the mind furnishes the evidence to explain its discontent. And the mind is truly brilliant at providing such evidence.

Imagine walking through a beautiful park on a spring day. You're happy, but then for some unknown reason a flicker of sadness ripples across your mind. It may be the result of hunger because you skipped lunch or perhaps you unwittingly triggered a troubling memory. After a few minutes you might start to feel a little down. As soon as you notice your lowered spirits you begin to probe yourself: It's a lovely day. It's a beautiful park. I wish I were feeling happier than I am now.

Think about that for a moment: I wish I were feeling happier. How do you feel now? You probably feel worse. This is because you focused on the gap between how you feel and how you want to feel. And focusing on the gap highlighted it. The mind sees the gap as a problem to be solved. This approach is disastrous when it comes to your emotions because of the intricate interconnection between your thoughts, emotions, and bodily sensations.

You begin to overthink; you start asking yourself endlessly the same questions that demand immediate answer: What's up with me today? I should be happy.

Your spirits sink a little deeper. Your body may tense up.

These sensations then feed back into your mind, which then feels even more threatened and a little more downbeat. If your spirits sink far enough, you'll start to become really preoccupied and miss the small, but beautiful things that would normally cheer you up: you might fail to notice the ducks playing on the lake, the innocent smiles of children.

Of course, nobody broods over problems because they believe it's a toxic way of thinking. People genuinely believe that if they worry enough over their unhappiness, they will eventually find a solution. They just need to make one last heave think a little more about the problem ... But research shows the opposite: in fact, brooding reduces our ability to solve problems; and it's absolutely hopeless for dealing with emotional difficulties.

The evidence is clear: brooding is the problem, not the solution.

### *Manage the vicious cycle*

You can't stop the triggering of unhappy memories, negative self-talk and judgmental ways of thinking - but what you can stop is what happens next. You can stop the vicious cycle from feeding off itself and triggering the next spiral of negative thoughts. And you can do this by harnessing an alternative way of relating to yourself and the world. The mind can do so much more than simply analyse problems with its' Doing' mode. The problem is that we use the 'Doing 'mode so much. Yet there is another way.

If you stop and reflect for a moment, the mind doesn't just think. It can also be aware that it is thinking. This form of pure awareness allows you to experience the world directly. It's bigger than thinking. It's like a high mountain a vantage point from which you can see everything for many miles around.

Pure awareness transcends thinking. It allows you to step outside the chattering negative self-talk and your reactive impulses and emotions. It allows you to look at the world once again with open eyes. And when you do so, a sense of wonder and quiet contentment begins to reappear in your life.

> Mindfulness isn't difficult, we just need to remember to do it.
>
> Sharon Salzberg

# Create Space

Life is full of challenges; it constantly tests our patience. Sometimes, we subconsciously react to difficulties based on patterns deeply embedded in our brain. The end result is not always positive. Patience, or the ability to endure discomfort, can be an effective strategy for choosing a rational response rather than an impulsive reaction. As an old saying goes, *"A moment of patience in a moment of anger saves you a thousand moments of regret."* While this applies to life in general, work is certainly no exception.

To better understand the neurology behind our patterns of reaction, it's useful to take a look at our triune brain.

### The Triune Brain

The human brain is made up of three parts and thus the term triune, which means three in one. Those three parts are the reptilian brain, the limbic brain, and the cortex. About 225 million years old, the reptilian brain formed during our early evolution and is the oldest part of the organ. The reptilian brain is focused on our basic needs for survival.

The next-oldest part of the brain, the limbic system, is about 170 million years old. When we began to be "caring beings" individuals concerned with the well-being of our offspring the limbic system was the cause. It's also the source of our feelings and moods.

The cortex was the last area of the brain to develop and it is 40 million years old. It's where we do our rational, intellectual, and logical thinking. It's the home of our conscious awareness.

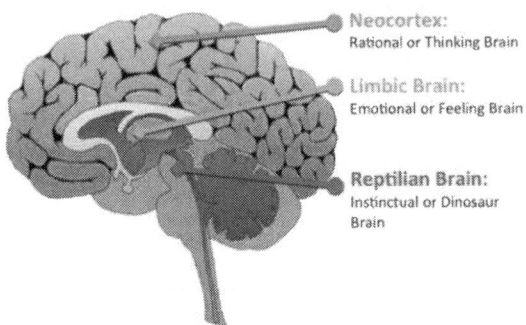

When we feel threatened, the amygdala- part of our limbic system triggers our "fight or flight" response. It's often called an amygdala hijack. The hijacking of the rational functioning of the rest of our brain, making our actions hard to control. In fight or flight mode, our bodies prepare either to physically defend ourselves against an imminent threat or run away.

The fight or flight reflex helped keep us to stay alive during our early evolution and can still do the same when we find ourselves in a dangerous situation. Although most of us rarely find ourselves in imminent physical danger today, life is still full of situations in which we feel threatened. Precisely because these situations rarely pose a physical danger, making a rational, conscious choice is better for our relationships, productivity, health, and wellbeing than making an automatic, subconscious decision.

Life is full of situations that "threaten" your schedule, your plans, your goals, or your intentions. Still, you don't have to let the ancient, reptilian part of your brain take control. You have evolved; you have a cortex. The cortex allows you to come up with logical and rational solutions the cortex offers patience.

By being aware of how your mind works, and your 'Doing' and your 'Being 'mode, you create that space that is going to allow you acknowledge when your amygdala is taking over and stay calm in the face of challenging situations. It's the ability to confront the situation directly and handle it sensibly, rather than on impulse.

While fight or flight attempts to solve problems, the space we create gives us the clarity needed to solve modern problems at the source: in the mind. We will talk more about how to create that space, but it is the right path to living a more effective life that's focused on the roots of problems instead of the symptoms.

Space and perspective don't come naturally to everyone, but it is a skill that can be developed and nurtured. With mindfulness practice, we start to perceive and process reality more through our cortex the -rational, intellectual, and logical part of our brains -and much less through our reptilian brain. We can then rewire our brain to create space and move away from autopilot.

### *Mindfulness At Work Quick Start -Create Space*

- Now that you understand how your brain works, the next time you face one of these situations where you can feel your amygdala kicking in, stop and take a breath to create space. That space that is going to allow you to see things with perspective and move away from autopilot.

- Now that you have created that space, decide your next step. Now you will decide instead of the limbic brain taking over and deciding on your behalf.

- Consider whether creating that space would be of benefit to you and why. Would it be beneficial at work or at home?

- Can you recall a situation when you reacted with your limbic brain, without filters, with your amygdala, and now you regret?

- How things could have been different now if you didn't react that way?

> Step outside for a while – calm your mind. It is better to hug a tree than to bang your head against a wall continually.
>
> Rasheed Ogunlaru

## Change is Here To Stay

Change is here to stay. And only resilience people and agile organisations will have a sustainable success.

Everything changes and we have all heard the saying, "The only constant in life is change." Yet, knowing it and effectively adopting it are two different things.

The human being is neurologically programmed to prefer things that are familiar. In fact, scientists estimate that 95 percent of our behaviours are based on habits and only 5 percent of what we do is based on conscious choice. Familiarity provides us with a greater sense of psychological safety.

When things do change, we feel like we're out of control. The inability to accept the reality that everything changes is one of the main reasons we create pain and suffering for ourselves. Mindfulness can be a powerful change management tool. It can help you rewire your brain to be more comfortable with change.

Learning to embrace the reality of constant change is a powerful thing. Building greater acceptance of the reality of constant change is a foundation for more balance, less stress, better health, and ultimately more peace of mind.

In most, if not all, work environments, change is constant processes-processes change, system change, people change, and so on.

The extent to we're able to manage these changes is critical to both our distract and our ability to realize our potential.

Mindfulness can help you manage the changes that are imposed externally and outside of your control.

**Let's start by understanding what resistance is**

Constantly scanning the environment, our subconscious mind takes in data from all our senses. As we have seen the subconscious is driven by self-preservation and if it perceives something in our environment as a threat, we're compelled to act. If it weren't for this process, we might not be alive. Thanks to this body reaction our ancestors could survive to many threats, like running away from a dinosaur or a mammoth.

Many organisations are going through restructuring or other types of changes. The way our subconscious responds to a restructuring at work in much the same way as we would have to an oncoming woolly mammoth. It's a survival instinct.

Because that is the way we are hardwired, even if the change is something we want, it requires effort to overcome our neurological impulse to keep things the same.

When we try to resist resistance, we only generate more of it. We create an inner battle that often leads to anger, frustration, stress, and anxiety. Resisting resistance doesn't help us move forward; instead, it negatively impacts both our health and well-being.

The key to managing resistance and therefore better managing change is to face it and embrace it. Embracing resistance is not only healthier, but it can also be instructing, enabling us to both accept change and become part of the solution in many cases which also give us a sense of relief.

**Welcoming Resistance**

The mindful approach to managing change outside of your control is to be aware of it, to accept it, and to learn from it. By observing your own resistance neutrally, you can create mental space from it, which can be the difference between automatically reacting to a perceived threat or deliberately responding in a constructive way.

Of course, there's a significant difference between acknowledging and observing resistance and overcome the negative emotions it evokes. Once you step back from the experience of resistance, it no longer has the same ability to cloud your mind and drain your energy.

Once you're able to observe your resistance, see whether there's anything you can learn from it. Are you resisting simply because of your natural preference for familiarity? Or are you resisting because something really doesn't make sense? Labelling and understanding the root cause of your resistance can be insightful.

With clarity of mind and a greater understanding of your resistance, you can mindfully respond. When you label and create that space you can choose to accept the change and let of your resistance, enabling you to move forward. Or you can choose to mindfully resist the change with focus and awareness instead of with your amygdala and your autopilot.

Although change is constant in our life and at work, managing change isn't easy. And that is the reason why almost 70 % of the initiatives in an organisation fail.

Because we usually focus on the change, which is external, and forget the transition, which is the emotional part of us that we need to change. We need to change our behaviour.

And to change our behaviour, we need motivation.

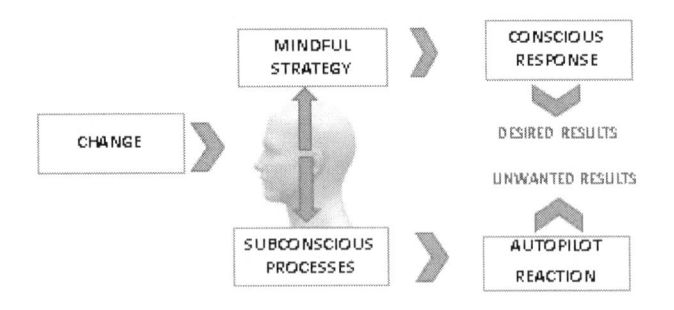

CHANGE → MINDFUL STRATEGY → CONSCIOUS RESPONSE → DESIRED RESULTS

SUBCONSCIOUS PROCESSES → AUTOPILOT REACTION → UNWANTED RESULTS

### *Acceptance is Key to Enhance Change*

Whether we like it or not we all resist to change because of the way of brain is wired.

Once you are aware, it is the first step to choose your reactions. As you can see, we are going back to awareness, which is the key for a mindful life.

Our motivations can come from both external and internal sources. When change is motivated purely by external sources—by force, with no internal acceptance, for example- people may change their behaviours, but most likely they'll also be resistant and resentful. This is driven by our brain and most people will do it automatically.

However, if an externally motivated change becomes internally accepted, the possibility to embrace the change is far greater.

With mindfulness, individuals can face and accept their own resistance to change. They can make a mindful choice either to embrace the change or mindfully resist it. Even mindful resistance can even enhance the change process.

If we apply mindfulness to the change process, we can face and embrace our resistance, optimizing outcomes for ourselves and others. We can cultivate both the motivation to move forward and the ability to realize desired results.

The only constant is change. And the only way we grow is by adapting and embracing change. When we resist change without mindfulness, we create unnecessary suffering for ourselves and others. When we embrace change with mindfulness, we're able to take action in the interest of improving our health, happiness, and realizing our potential. When we resist mindfully and manage change with mindfulness, we move forward, we learn, we develop, we maintain balance, and we optimize outcomes for both ourselves and others.

### *Mindfulness At Work Quick Start- Change Management*

1. Be aware of change. Simply acknowledge it and familiarize yourself with it to create some familiarity.

2. Be aware of your feelings and resistance – Remember that if you resist is OK. The important is to do it mindfully if you choose to.

3. Observe your feelings. Try to understand where it comes from. It could be a powerful learning experience. Is it coming from past experiences? Is it coming from fear to what might happen next?

4.You have created space. And this space will help to make a mindful choice. This may mean you choose to fully embrace the change and let go of any resistance it could be that you choose to influence or if could mean that you choose to not to accept the change. Doesn't matter. The most important is to make the choice with a clear mind

5. Take action in your area of control. As we mentioned we are habitual beings so any change will take time. But the most important is to take small steps and move forward. And remember, you don't need to make the transition on your own. You can also identify what type of support you might need.

In a reality where change is here to stay, mindfully embracing change is one of the most powerful benefits of the mindfulness practice.

> The little things? The little moments? They aren't little.
>
> Jon Kabat-Zinn

## Autopilot

Our autopilot may be inconvenient, but it is not a mistake.

Our minds have a bottleneck in the so-called 'working memory' that allows us to keep only a few simple things in them at any one time. As soon as you exceed this threshold, items tend to be forgotten.

If there's too much information in the mind, your 'working memory' begins to overflow. You begin to feel stressed. You begin to feel powerless and your mind starts periodically 'freezing', making you indecisive and increasingly unaware of what's going on around you. You become forgetful, and exhausted. It's similar to the way a computer gets slower and slower as you open more and more windows. At first, you don't notice the impact but, gradually, once you cross an invisible threshold, the computer becomes slower, until it freezes before finally crashing.

In the short term, the automatic pilot allows us to extend the working memory by creating habits. If we repeat something more than a couple of times, the mind links together all of the actions needed to complete a task in a brilliantly seamless manner. Many of the tasks we carry out each day are phenomenally complex, requiring the co-ordination of dozens of muscles and the firing of thousands of nerves. But they can all be linked together using a habit that consumes only a small part of your brainpower (and an even smaller proportion of your awareness). The brain can easily chain such habits together to carry out long, complex tasks with very little input from the conscious mind at all.

**Mindfulness and your autopilot**

Have you ever turned on your computer to send an email, only to get distracted into answering some others, and then turned your computer off again an hour later without sending the original message?

This is not what you had intended to do. But notice the consequence: when you next turn on your computer, you'll still have to send your original message, and you will also have to look at all the new messages in response to that one hour of unscheduled work.

When this happens, you may think you are doing a good job just 'clearing the junk tasks' – but what you've actually done is to make the email system speed up!

Mindfulness does not say, 'Don't send emails', but it may remind you to check in with yourself and ask, 'Is this what I had intended to be doing?'

As the years pass, this can become a huge problem as you cede more and more control of your life to the autopilot including much of what you think.

Habits trigger thoughts, which trigger more thoughts, which end up triggering yet more habitual thoughts. Fragments of negative thoughts and feelings can form themselves into patterns which amplify your emotions. Before you know it, you can become overwhelmed by deep-seated stresses, anxieties, and sadness's. And by the time you've noticed the unwanted thoughts and feelings, they'll have become too strong to contain. A thoughtless' comment by a friend can leave you feeling unhappy and insecure.

You may desperately try and head off the spiral of stress by trying to suppress it. You might try arguing with yourself, telling yourself: I'm stupid for feeling like this. But such thinking about thoughts, feelings and emotions simply makes them worse. Very soon the autopilot can become overloaded with too many windows left open. Your mind slows down. Your thoughts, memories, anxieties, and tasks - just like a computer with too many windows open.

Your mind slows down. You may become exhausted, anxious, frantic, and chronically dissatisfied or even crash.

When you reach the point where such overload has seized the conscious mind, it's very difficult to reverse the process simply by thinking your way out, for this is like opening yet another program on the computer, overlaying it with yet another window.

Instead, you need to find a way of stepping outside the cycle almost as soon as you notice it's begun.

This is the first step in learning to deal with life more skilfully. It involves training yourself to notice when your autopilot is taking over, so that you can then make a choice about what you want your mind to be focusing upon. You need to learn to close down some of the programs that have been left running in the background of your mind.

The first stage of regaining your innate mindfulness involves returning to basics. You need to relearn how to focus your awareness on one thing at a time.

# COLLABORATING WITH YOUR MIND

Your actions are your only true belongings.

Allan Lokos

# Mindfully Controlling Your Action Addiction

The natural reaction to something you like is wanting more, and the reaction to something you don't like is to try to push it away.

Think of the last time you ate a nice piece of chocolate or something else you really like. Were you satisfied after the first bite and put the rest down, or did you want more to the extent that your thoughts were already consumed by taking the next bite? Try to imagine you are offered a nice piece of chocolate, and just before you put your teeth into it, it is taken out of your hands and thrown away. How do you feel?

This is a natural reaction pattern, and it can be explained by looking at one of the brain's neurochemical processes, particularly our production of, and desire for, dopamine.

### *Dopamine Rush*

Neurotransmitters are chemicals that transmit signals between brain cells. Two of the most important neurotransmitters are dopamine and serotonin. Together, they account for the "attraction/ rejection" reactions we experience in day-to-day life.

Dopamine is a reward substance that causes us to feel joy, satisfaction, and fulfilment. Every time we get something we like, the brain releases dopamine. It makes us feel good. It's the reason why, after having something we like, we want more. While dopamine can be nice for obvious reasons, it also has a dark side: dopamine is addictive. All forms of addiction whether to gambling, drugs, overeating, or praise from your boss—are based on the desire for a dopamine rush.

If praise is your drug of choice, each pat on the back you receive is accompanied by a release of dopamine. And much of your energy and effectiveness are likely dependent on attaining things you like, as well as avoiding things you dislike.

Fortunately, we can actually avoid falling victim to our own dopamine addictions. Another neurotransmitter, serotonin, has a wide-ranging impact on the mind and body, primarily serving to inhibit impulsive behaviour and increase relaxation and clarity.

**Your Freedom-Serotonin**

Serotonin and dopamine are closely connected. Serotonin balances out the negative effect of dopamine, enabling us to be more resilient in the face of adversity, be that criticism or even physical or emotional pain.

So how can we create more serotonin and experience more peace and freedom as a result? Research shows mindfulness practice to be one way to increase the levels of serotonin in your brain.

When you stop yourself from following an impulse -like quitting after one serving of your favourite food or drink- serotonin balances out the dopamine release. In your daily mindfulness practice, you're constantly resisting impulses to follow distracting thoughts or hold onto stress. You're training your ability to observe your own experiences, giving you the mental space to deliberately choose responses rather than react on autopilot. Every time you successfully inhibit automatic reactions, your serotonin level increases.

This way you can enjoy the things you truly enjoy without developing addiction. It means you can respond more skilfully to things you don't like without becoming angry and aggressive. You attain greater balance.

Once you start regular mindfulness practice, you will notice an increase in calm and a decrease in impulsive reactions. The more you train yourself to resist automatic impulses, the more in balance your dopamine and serotonin levels become. And balance is genuine freedom, freedom that comes from within.

***Mindfulness At Work Quick Start - Freedom of Choice***

When you feel an impulse to pursue something you like, pause for a moment to let your serotonin balance out any release of dopamine.

**Use the STOP Mindfulness Technique**

The STOP Technique is a mindfulness-based practice designed to help you defuse stress in the moment.

Creating space in the day to pause, slow down a racing mind, and get back into the present moment has been shown to be incredibly helpful in reducing the negative effects of stress.

Taking a brief pause—even for less than one minute—can help you gain perspective and determine the best possible action you can take next.

Over time and with practice, this way of responding becomes a habit. As Sharon Salzberg says, "Mindfulness isn't difficult, we just need to remember to do it."

**Stop**

Interrupt your thoughts with the command 'stop!' and pause whatever you're doing.

**Take a Breath**

Notice your breathing for a second. Breathe in slowly through the nose, expanding the belly, and exhale slowly and deeply through pursed lips.

**Observe**

Become the observer of your thoughts, emotions, and physical reactions. What thoughts do you notice? What emotions are present? How does your body feel? Tune in and sit with whatever arises for a few moments.

**Proceed**

Mindfully consider how you'd like to respond. What's one thing you can focus on right now? What's your most important and urgent priority? Narrow down your focus and take it one small step at a time.

Freedom is a state of mind. Not a place. Not a situation. Freedom releases a flow of mental space and effectiveness.

Wherever you go, there you are.

Jon Kabat-Zinn

## Collaborating With Your Mind

Most people, after practising Mindfulness, they have a sense of relief and control. The way most people describe it is that it creates 'space' between what happens and your own chosen response.

In today's 'always on' culture most people are victims of their own automatic reactions.

What can change during that 'space'? Everything.

That 'space 'gives you the freedom to control your thoughts, your actions, and, more profoundly, your life.

In this chapter we will review our natural cognitive tendencies, the effect these tendencies have on productivity, and some simple but very powerful rules for increasing mental effectiveness.

### *Are You In Control?*

Life is about results. Results come from our actions. Our actions come from the choices we make. Our choices come from the thoughts we think. It works like this:

MIND › CHOICES › ACTIONS › RESULTS

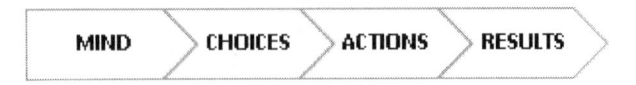

Our thoughts are the foundation for everything we want to achieve in life, hence the importance of collaborating with your mind because simply said, your results-your future-depends on it. When our mind is clear and focused, we are in a better position to manage our thoughts. This is true in all aspects of life, but especially true in the workplace.

According to research, however, on average our mind is wandering almost half of our time. We are constantly thinking about events that happened in the past, or might happen in the future, rather than attending to what's happening right now. This limits our ability to achieve meaningful results.

Does it sound familiar?

So, you may ask yourself. If it's true that our thoughts shape our future, and I am not present to take control of my thoughts: Who's making the decisions in my life?

Ah, Ah!

The natural tendency for our mind to wander has worsened over the past few decades during what we call the digital era. The digital era supposedly was going to help with many tasks at hand, but we've gone from handling a typewriter and a telephone to juggling e-mails, texts, tweets, spreadsheets, reports, deadlines, and much more all at the same time.

And the same is happening to the new generations. If you have children, you can easily see that either at school or Uni they have all have these "digital" interruptions. And, like change, this is not only going to stay, but to increase.

**Multitasking is a Weakness**

We are now experiencing distractions and information overload all the time. According to the former director of the Accenture Institute of Strategic Change, Tom Davenport, "Understanding and managing attention is now the single most important determinant of business success."

We are living in an "attention economy" where the ability to manage our attention and the quality of our attention is key to our success. But in the digital era, our attention is at risk.

Researchers studying the mind's natural tendency to wander calculated that on average our mind wanders 46.9 percent of the time. In other words, while we are at work, 53.1 percent of the time our mind is on task. The rest of the time it is off task.

Can you, your children, or your team be off task 46.9 % of the time?

Imagine the positive impact you could have in your life and work by increasing, even if slightly, that percentage. Imagine the results in your business.

Attention, in the digital age, is becoming a new enabler of business performance.

Researchers have found that the brain tries to attend to all our distractions all at the same time. It defaults to multitasking. And you know what? Multitasking is a myth.

When we try to multitask, the research shows, we take more time, make more mistakes, and use up more mental energy.

We always thought we could pay attention to more than one thing at a time. And that is true for activities that do not require attention. That is, without conscious thought. For example, we can jog and talk at the same time.

However, from a neurological perspective, we're not capable of focusing attention on two things at the same time. When we think we are multitasking, what we are doing in reality is shift tasking.

In the context of multitasking at work, researchers have found that "multitaskers are masters of everything that is irrelevant, they let themselves be distracted by anything."

The reality is, as amazing and powerful as our brains are, we're not capable of focusing our attention on two things at the same time

Studies have shown that multitasking lowers people's job satisfaction, damages personal relationships, adversely affects memory, and negatively impacts health. Multitasking reduces effectiveness because it takes longer to complete tasks and leads to more mistakes. This is because when we switch our focus from one task to another, it takes time to make the shift. Depending on the complexity of the new task, that can take anywhere from a few seconds to several minutes. This phenomenon is called shift-time. Shift-time saps our mental energy and taxes our productivity.

Researchers from Harvard Business School discovered that multitasking also affects creativity.

The problem we have with multitasking, and why so many do it, is because is addictive. Shifting rapidly back and forth between tasks and getting things done, even if without quality, feels exciting. This is because multitasking provides a "dopamine injection" to the brain. As we have seen, dopamine is a naturally produced neurotransmitter in the brain that is directly linked to addiction. It gives you instant gratification, so your brain is constantly looking for a new dopamine kick, like a sugar high. Unfortunately, that sugar high is usually followed by a sugar crash.

The good news is that there is a way to break the habit.

**Mindfulness is About You**

It's about overcoming the multitasking trap and creating that space between your wandering mind and external distractions. It's about being the best version of yourself every day. It's about generating greater mental effectiveness so that you can reach your full potential, both on a professional and a personal level. Effectiveness in this context is the ability to achieve your goals, objectives, and wishes in life.

You can create that mind in balance, which sees reality clearly and values ethics. A balanced mind is relaxed, focused, and clear. And when you are in this state, you are aware of your circumstances and choose your actions.

And as you know now, by choosing your actions you create your future.

**The Impact**

Mindfulness has a positive impact on our physiology, mental processes, and work performance. At the physiological level, researchers have demonstrated that mindfulness practice can result in a stronger immune system, lower blood pressure, and a lower heart rate. People sleep better and feel less stressed.

Mindfulness increases the density of grey cells in our cerebral cortex, the part of the brain that thinks rationally and solves problems. Cognitive function improves, resulting in better memory, increased concentration, reduced cognitive rigidity, and faster reaction times. Not surprisingly, people who practice mindfulness techniques report an overall increase in quality of life.

Other researchers have found similar benefits from mindfulness practice in corporate contexts, including:

- Increased creativity and innovation.
- Improved employer-employee relations.
- Reduced absenteeism due to illness; and
- improved ethical decision-making.

Mindfulness is ultimately a tool for developing a highly functional and effective mind.

### *Neuroplasticity*

Training our brain is possible because of what's scientifically termed neuroplasticity. In short, neuroplasticity describes the structural flexibility of our brains, including the ability to create new neural pathways through practice and repetition.

Anything we do becomes easier to do again, because our brains create new and stronger neural connections every time, we do it. We can keep learning and growing and effectively rewiring our brain throughout our entire lives.

Successful people are not made from a different cloth. They create habits and are consistent until they master them.

You can as well.

Let's talk about the basis of Mindfulness

**The Basis of Mindfulness**

In Mindfulness At Work, we are trying to achieve mental effectiveness and there are two basic rules that help you manage your focus and awareness so you can improve results (doing less!) and improve your well-being.

**Rule #1: Mindfully Choose and Focus**

Making your choice is important but actually staying focused on your choice, object, or activity is the first rule of mental effectiveness. A focused mind helps you be more calmed, productive, and aware of your surroundings which also leads to a better emotional intelligence. When you are focused, you are fully present, you excel in whatever you are doing, and you turn off your autopilot and multitasking mode.

To get there we need to start acknowledging that the majority of distractions are irrelevant and can be set aside in the moment. Most of your thoughts are mental clutter. Being aware of our internal and external distractions help choosing where to focus your attention.

As simple as it sounds, Rule #1 is a powerful way to increase productivity and effectiveness.

Choose your distractions. Choose the time thieves at work. I am sure when you think about time thieves, there are one or two people (or more!) coming to your mind!

You have also probably been distracted by an email when you were in the middle of preparing an important presentation. All of the sudden you see the email alert, you open it, and when you realise, you have spent the last 30 minutes 'reacting' to someone's agenda instead of focusing on what is important. Familiar?

Most of us work in a team or with customers, so that is why we need a second rule

### Rule #2:  Observe and Choose Your Distractions

There are distractions and distractions.  Of course, some distractions do require you to take immediate actions, especially when it is an emergency or a call from your boss…

The importance of this rule is creating that space that allows you to observe and choose your next action depending on your priorities at hand.

Rule #2 ensures you work in a focused way while remaining aware of distractions and you have freedom of choice.

When you apply both rules, you have three options for responding to any distraction:

1. You can observe it and choose not to deal with the distraction because it doesn't add any value. You will refocus on your activity.

2. You can observe it and decide when you are going to deal with it. You will refocus on your activity.

3. You can observe it, check your priorities, and choose to focus on this activity. You assign your present task a time in the future.

We all have long list of tasks, projects, meetings…etc. so these 2 rules give you the awareness, freedoms, and choice to focus on what matters most. most at that specific timeframe.

**How to Apply Both Rules**

We often find ourselves in situations in which we apply one rule but not the other.

Rasmund Hougaard, founder of Potential Project, explains these 2 rules with this matrix.

As the first quadrant shows, when you are focused but on autopilot, mostly described as being in "flow. "Flow is characterized by some degree of absorption and therefore lacking awareness of external distractions. This can pose a problem even during routine work because you may neglect sensory signals of important events around you or physiological signals indicating you need rest, movement, or food. We need awareness to pick up on relevant distractions like our boss coming into our office or signals from our body. Although many things can be done on autopilot, most of the time it is beneficial to remain aware of our surroundings.

In the fourth quadrant, you're aware but easily distracted. Some people find that they come up with more creative ideas in this quadrant. But if your mind is too distracted, you'll have difficulty retaining any good ideas.

In the third quadrant, you're neither focused nor aware. Some people see this quadrant as the most relaxing. It's obviously not a very useful state of mind in a work context.

In the second quadrant defined as "mindful" we have the greatest mental bandwidth to complete tasks and the highest quality of interactions with our environment and other people. The second quadrant equates to being present with ourselves and what we're doing. It's the best response to the digital age and a way of improving your performance in an attention economy.

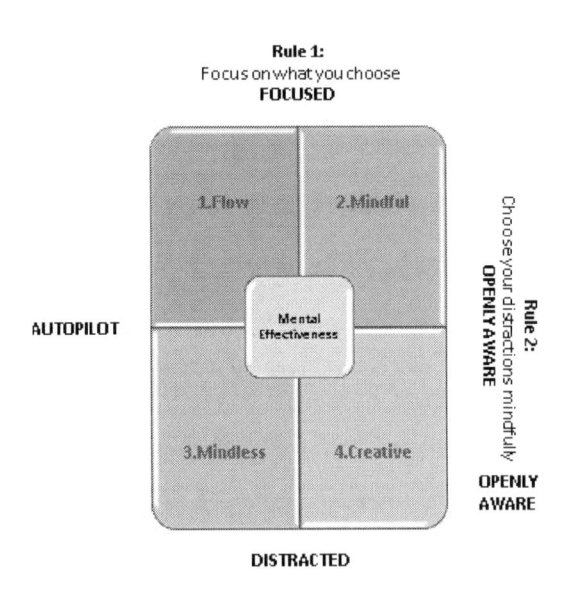

## Overcoming Obstacles

If you're used to multitasking, you'll be tempted again and again to try to do more than one thing at a time. Every time you catch yourself, pause and then choose to maintain focus on one thing. After a while, you'll create new neural connections and form new habits.

The other big challenge many people encounter is their co-workers, work culture, and office layout, especially in open-office environments. Many organizations operate with implicit assumptions around availability and urgency. Although people being available and able to respond to urgent tasks is fundamental to business success, it needs to be balanced.

**Mindful Work**

Combining the two rules of mental effectiveness focus on what you choose and choose your distractions mindfully results in a new way of working that can truly optimize individual performance. The key elements of the two rules are straightforward: give full conscious attention to whatever you're doing at the moment.

Maintaining focus and choosing your distractions wisely allows you to actively choose your response to events in your inner and outer worlds instead of reacting on autopilot.

These two rules help strip away the noise and disruptions that can clutter your mind and side-track you on the way to attaining your goals.

In the remainder part of the book, I'll share how you can apply what you've learned in this chapter to crucial elements of your work life. I will share useful mental and work technique that, when used, help you to declutter your mind, increaser results and improve your well-being.

> You cannot control the results, only your actions.
>
> Allan Lokos

## Work as an adult, observe as a child

In my experience, looking at things from a different perspective, with fresh eyes, is key for business success.

Before we get into new work techniques is important, we talk about this matter.

Without the ability to be opened to look at things from a different angle, we get into 'I have always done it this way' defensive mode, and we don't want to get out of our comfort zone. We might become complacent with the way we run our life and business and we might just wake up to find ourselves missing the train.

In mindfulness, we call the ability to see things with a fresh perspective "the beginner's mind. And if you really want to make a change, I encourage you to look at things with the beginner's mind. Be open.

However, it is easier said than done.

A few natural traits stand between each of us and a beginner's mind: namely, habitual perception and cognitive rigidity.

### *I Know It All*

In our interactions with other people, our work, and ourselves, we often limit ourselves to restricted perceptions to what we know and have known. We become cognitively rigid.

We get used to see things. A flower, the nature, our art, our creations…

In evolution, this is called pattern recognition, and it represents one of the greatest strengths of the human mind.

However, the automatic association between what's actually in front of you and what you've seen in the past- the neurological process called habitual perception- can be problematic. It means you often don't actually see what's right there in front of you. You look but you don't see.

Because, again, we go in autopilot.

In fact, what you do see has much less to do with actual reality, and much more to do with the reality that your mind creates based on your history and habits. In other words, you have programmed yourself to see reality in a certain way.

Cognitive rigidity- the inflexibility created by automatically recalling our habitual perceptions -it doesn't help us innovate. On the contrary, cognitive rigidity affects our effectiveness and performance, both personally and professionally.

Thankfully, seeing things with a beginner's mind can be a proactive choice and this is the reason we start with this before we get into other techniques.

Albert Einstein is known to have said, "A problem cannot be solved with the same level of mind that created it."

At work and at home, how often do the same challenges come up time and time again?

What if, instead of seeing these challenges the same way every time, we viewed them with fresh eyes? Would we confront those challenges more effectively?

Mindfulness practice helps you to create the space, being aware of the habitual patterns and allowing you to choose to see things as they actually are.

With a beginner's mind, we see things with fresh eyes and an open mind.

### *Mindfulness At Work Quick Start - Beginner's Mind*

Challenge yourself to be more curious in your day-to-day activities.

For one week, take you time, stop, create space and when looking at a problem or project at work ask yourself

- What could that mean?
- What if I do this differently?

And if you are brave enough, ask someone completely neutral and away from your professional network (a friend, your partner and depending on their age even your children)

- What do you think of XXXX?
- Could you give me your feedback about XXX?

Cultivating a beginner's mind can be a wonderful way to change how you experience life. Regardless of your work environment, daily life can be filled with more wonders and possibilities when you see things with a fresh perspective.

And like everything else, the choice is yours

Wisdom says we are nothing. Love says we are everything. Between these two our life flows.

Jack Kornfield

## Mindfulness and Its Benefits

Can you remember the last time you lay in bed wrestling become calm, to just be quiet, so that you could get some sleep? But whatever you tried seemed to fail. Every time you forced yourself not to think, your thoughts exploded into life with renewed strength. You told yourself not to worry, but suddenly discovered countless new things to worry about. You tried fluffing up the pillow and rolling over to get more comfortable, but soon enough, you began thinking again. As the night ground ever onwards, your strength progressively drained away, leaving you feeling fragile and broken. By the time the alarm went off, you were exhausted, bad tempered and thoroughly miserable.

Throughout the next day you had the opposite problem – you wanted to be wide awake, but could hardly stop yawning. You stumbled into work, but weren't really present. You couldn't concentrate. Your eyes were red and puffy. Your whole body ached, and your mind felt empty.

You'd stare at the pile of papers on your desk for ages, hoping something, anything, would turn up and contentment so that you could gather enough momentum to do a day's work.

In meetings, you could barely keep your eyes open, let alone con begun to slip through your fingers ... you felt ever-more anxious, stressed, and exhausted.

Familiar?

It's a secret that was well understood in the ancient world and is kept alive in some cultures even today. But many of us in the Western world have largely forgotten how to live a good and joyful existence. And it's often even worse than this. We try so hard to be happy that we end up missing the most important parts happiness, peace and contentment can be found and how you can rediscover them for yourself.

Mindfulness will teach you how to free yourself progressively from anxiety, stress, unhappiness, and exhaustion. I am not promising eternal bliss; everyone experiences periods of pain and suffering and it's naive and dangerous to pretend otherwise. And yet, it is possible to taste an alternative to the relentless struggle that pervades much of our daily lives.

In the following pages and in the accompanying Mindfulness At Work Program, should you choose to accept it, I offer a series of simple practices that you can incorporate into your daily life and work.

### *Let's start talking about the benefits in your health*

Because we are holistic beings, even if this book is for Mindfulness at Work, let start but talking about the benefits in your health:

- Numerous psychological studies have shown that mindful people are happier and more contented than average. These are some of the benefits of Mindfulness practice

- Anxiety, depression, and irritability all decrease with regular sessions of meditation. Memory also improves, reaction times become faster and mental and physical stamina increase.

- Regular meditators enjoy better and more fulfilling relationships.

- Studies worldwide have found that meditation reduces the key indicators of chronic stress, including hypertension.

- Meditation has also been found to be effective in reducing the impact of serious conditions, such as chronic pain and cancer, and can even help to relieve drug and alcohol dependence.

- Studies have now shown that meditation bolsters the immune system and thus helps to fight off colds, flu, and other diseases.

### *What are the benefits of mindfulness At Work?*

*"Mindfulness should no longer be considered a "nice-to-have" for executives. It's a "must-have: a way to keep our brains healthy, to support self-regulation and effective decision-making capabilities, and to protect ourselves from toxic stress. It can be integrated into one's religious or spiritual life or practiced as a form of secular mental training. When we take*

*a seat, take a breath, and commit to being mindful, particularly when we gather with others who are doing the same, we have the potential to be changed."*

-Harvard Business Review

Alongside the overall benefit of improved performance that comes from mindfulness, there are several other benefits that contribute to overall well-being at work:

**Reduces Stress & Anxiety**

Mindfulness makes perfect sense for dealing with stress and anxiety because it takes you out of fight-or-flight mode and brings you into a relaxed state of mental clarity and calm. By becoming more aware of your thoughts and body, you can better assess and identify your feelings and approach them in a more positive way. Scientifically, Mindfulness practice reduces activity in the stress initiating part of your brain called the amygdala.

**Improves your Focus**

Studies show that mindfulness can improve your ability to focus on one thing at a time and help curb our tendency for distraction. This ability to focus will start to translate to everything you do. It helps you to avoid multi-tasking and places an emphasis on monotasking. A focused mind is a productive mind.

**Enhances Creativity**

Creativity greatly depends on your mental state. Mindfulness helps you to get into a creative frame of mind by combatting the negative thoughts that hinder creative thinking and self-expression. The fact that mindfulness focuses on the present helps you to think freely and creatively and allows your mind the space to bounce off ideas.

**Increases Emotional Intelligence and Resilience**

Mindfulness helps increase emotional intelligence in three major ways: It improves your ability to comprehend your own emotions; It helps you learn how to recognize the emotions of other people around you; It strengthens your ability to govern and control your emotions. He also notes that mindfulness improves a person's ability to use their emotions effectively by helping them determine which emotions are beneficial when undertaking certain activities.

**Improves Communication**

We live in a world full of distractions. With the constant influx of texts, tweets, and IM's, many of us have lost our ability to actively listen and be present. By incorporating mindfulness into your day, you can retrain yourself to focus on the present moment and truly listen to people with compassion and kindness. Not only does this have a positive impact on the people around you, but it also makes your day more interesting because you are engaging in active conversations with people and learning about them.

**Mindfulness & ROI**

So, can pursuing mindfulness be good for the bottom line? In David Gelles' *Mindful Work,* he delves into the subject of mindfulness in business, revealing evidence to support its benefits and real-world examples of companies who are seeing results.

As seen, bringing mindfulness to the workplace has the potential to decrease people's stress and anxiety through heightened awareness, which in turn leads to improved performance. Also, perhaps most importantly from a leadership perspective, mindfulness encourages engagement. Being fully present as a leader— and allowing your team to be fully in the moment — will reward both personally and professionally.

Despite these proven benefits, however, many people are still wary when they heard the word meditation.

So, before we proceed, it might be helpful to clear up some myths:

- Mindfulness is not a religion. Mindfulness is simply a method of mental training.

- Meditation is a way to practice Mindfulness, and most probably the most popular, but there are many other ways .As a matter of fact to practice mindfulness you only need yourself and your attention to the present moment. How you get there, it is up to you.

- Many people who practise meditation are themselves religious, but then again, many atheists and agnostics are keen meditators too.

- Mindfulness practice does not take a lot of time, although some patience and persistence are required. Many people soon find that mindfulness liberates them from the pressures, so they have more of it to spend on other things

- Mindfulness it not complicated. Nor is it about 'success' or 'failure'. Even when meditation feels difficult, you'll have learned something valuable about the workings of the mind and thus have benefited psychologically.

- It will not deaden your mind or prevent you from striving towards important career or lifestyle goals; nor will it trick you into falsely adopting a Pollyanna attitude to life. Mindfulness is not about accepting the unacceptable. It is about seeing the world with greater clarity so that you can take wiser and more considered action to change those things which need to be changed. Meditation helps cultivate a deep and compassionate awareness that allows you to assess your goals and find the optimum path towards realising your deepest values.

- Actually, Mindfulness will help you focus and achieve more of what is important and helps you to eliminate unnecessary things.

So, how can you start?

Like any other habit, enhancing your awareness, focus and attention is a habit, so you need to start taking small steps at a time.

And this book will guide you towards this journey.

> Live the actual moment. Only this actual moment is life.
>
> Thích Nhất Hạnh

# Let's Go To The Gym

So far, we've spent a significant amount of time understanding what is happening to our life, understanding our mind, demystifying mindfulness and understanding its benefits.

At its core, mindfulness is about going to the mental gym and moment by moment rewiring the neurological pathways of your brain. Mindfulness is a training. It is work, but a very pleasant kind of work.

Mindfulness practice is an investment. And it takes effort. Depending on what type of mindfulness you decide to embark, it takes time as well. Or not. Remember that meditation is a way of mindfulness but are many others. The simplest one is to be aware, focus and present. And that doesn't take time.

And while many would argue they have no time for mindfulness practice because they are busy, I see it very differently. Mindfulness practice is increasingly important to me, the busier I get. The more things I need to do, the more time I train. That's my way of ensuring I can stay focused, calm, and effective and not let the busyness clutter my mind.

This part of the book is about training your mind before you can actually introduce Mindfulness Ay Work.

Let's begin

*What would it be like if I could accept life – accept this moment – exactly as it is?*

Tara Brach

## Nam-Tok

Some of us struggle with leaving thoughts behind when we move from one task to the next. Still others have difficulties transitioning from work to home.

Mindfulness can strengthen your ability to let go of a thought before it leads to more related thoughts. In a way, it's similar to how your computer performs better after you've cleaned up the hard drive or emptied the cache. Letting go reduces the clutter in your mind.

One Tibetan word eloquently describes the challenge of letting go: nam-tok.

Imagine you are lying on a beach a long way from home. Suddenly, a thought about a work responsibility comes into your mind. This is a nam, a standalone thought that occurs in the mind.

But the mind rarely stops there.

Tok is the Tibetan word for each thought that spontaneously occurs as a result of the first thought. If your work nam started with a looming deadline, the related toks might have to do with approaching milestones or tasks yet to be completed. There are often several toks that arise with each nam. In fact, there can be a whole cascade of additional thoughts, depending on how our mind reacts to the initial nam.

Letting go is a simple but very powerful mental strategy. The following are a few ways you can better cultivate your ability to let go.

**Mindfulness At Work Quick Start - Managing Nam-Tok**

- Let's start identifying those Nams

- When you detect that thought, that Nam, isolate I before the toks begin to multiply. Imagine them like monkeys if it helps!

- Observe it, label it, and let it pass. And move one and refocus on the present.

- At the beginning, one of the main obstacles are expectations. Let go of your expectations about results. Let go of everything. Just be present.

- If it helps to refocus, use a breathing exercise to help you let go of thoughts and be in the moment one breath at a time.

- I will refer quite often to breathing so I have included an easy breathing exercise in the Annex but there are many others you can use!

> Meditation practice isn't about trying to throw ourselves away and become something better. It's about befriending who we are already.
>
> Pema Chödrön

## The Present

Two minutes with someone who's fully present is more powerful and effective than ten minutes with a distracted person.

Just think about the last time you were mindfully listened to. Unfortunately, nowadays is a luxury.

Being truly present requires you to fully engage with your current situation be it a meeting, at a meal, or while reading a book.

### The Present is Real

The past already happened. The future hasn't yet started. Nevertheless, our minds tend to wander between the two. At times, we all have trouble being present in the here and now.

Most people are familiar with the term Attention Deficit Hyperactivity Disorder (ADHD) a psychiatric condition in which individuals have significant problems maintaining focus. Fewer, though, are familiar with Attention Deficit Trait (ADT) an unrecognized, though quite real, phenomenon in which brain overload causes individuals to become easily distracted and impatient.

According to researchers, ADHD has a genetic component that can be exacerbated by hectic surroundings. ADT, however, is determined only by surroundings. Nobody is born predisposed to ADT; rather, it's a direct result of our interactions with today's high pressure, technology driven reality. ADT is a product of modern life. It is created by demands on our time and awareness that have exploded over the past two decades. When our minds are filled with noise, our brains lose the ability to be completely present.

Because of the many distractions in our lives both internal and external ADT is endemic to many workplaces, causing even the highest performers to struggle with time management, organization, and prioritizing tasks.

From a neurological perspective, people are experiencing a constant neural merry-go-round in the brain.

Being present in the moment is the best way to get the most out of your precious time. If you are not present, you are not here and you're trying to multitask. And multitasking, as I established in the previous chapters, is a myth. You just can't do multiple cognitive tasks at the same time.

None of us can.

Being present helps you be more intentional about what you do and how you live your life. It helps you be the best, most effective version of yourself.

Being present in the moment doesn't require a change in what you do. It requires a change in how you pay attention to what you do. It's a conscious decision to be present in the moment.

In reality, there is only now.

There is no other time: no past or future. The only time we get anything done is in this moment.

Mindfulness or Mindfulness meditation is not ten minutes of awareness. Mindfulness is awareness of every breath during all time you are present.

Being present is the path. If you focus on the target, you've missed the moment. If you focus on the path, you've reached the target.

### *Mindfulness At Work Quick Start – Be Present*

- Think about the last time you were not present in a meeting or not present having a conversation with a loved one. What did you miss? How did you feel?
- Make a conscious decision to intentionally be more present with a colleague, with a client, at a meeting, or at home. And notice what you feel.
- If you are at work, stop looking at your computer or phone if it is not absolutely necessary
- At home, when you are having dinner, having a conversation with your children or partner, leave your screens behind. Notice what you feel. Notice how they feel.

> If you want to conquer the anxiety of life, live in the moment, live in the breath.
>
> Amit Ray

## Awareness and Laser Focus

Mindfulness isn't about having less responsibilities It's not about eliminating everyday busyness or becoming more organized. Rather, it is about seeing distractions for what they are and not letting them take control.

Some research show improvements averaging 15 percent in ability to maintain focus when you train between five to seven days a week for ten minutes.

What I call **laser focus is the ability to concentrate on thoughts and tasks of your choice**. Creating mental clarity can help the busiest of us thrive, even in high-pressure environments filled with distractions.

***Awareness is the ability to observe your mind***.

Enhancing awareness helps you in becoming familiar with the workings of the mind and how that causes us to experience challenges in life. Awareness helps you not be a victim of circumstance only able to react automatically to situations as they develop. Awareness involves practice for a new kind of relationship with your thoughts and the world around you, allowing you to create that ´space 'between you and your reactions, regardless of the situation. With awareness, autopilot is no longer the default response mechanism. Instead, it brings a whole new sense of clarity and direction into your life and work.

Like many things in life, training your awareness and focus is simple, but not effortless. Our thoughts just aren't always easy to manage. Success in enhancing your focus and awareness is the ability to manage your wandering mind with relaxation, focus, and clarity. It's being able to concentrate in the midst of distraction and create that ´space´ from whatever might try to take your attention.

**Enhance Your Awareness and Focus**

Mindfulness practice is not passive. It's an active intervention in your brain's neural network.

Enhancing awareness helps you in becoming familiar with the workings of the mind and how that causes us to experience challenges in life. Awareness helps you not be a victim of circumstance only able to react automatically to situations as they develop. Awareness involves practice for a new kind of relationship with your thoughts and the world around you, allowing you to create that ´space 'between you and your reactions, regardless of the situation. With awareness, autopilot is no longer the default response mechanism. Instead, it brings a whole new sense of clarity and direction into your life and work.

For every moment you maintain focus, you create new "focus" neural connections and abilities. Thanks to neuroplasticity, the more you train, the stronger these neural connections and pathways become and the easier it becomes to stay focused.

This, however, doesn't happen overnight.

Awareness and Focus go together. Laser focus alone can be blind. The awareness gives laser focus, direction, and intentionality. Together, laser focus and awareness can help you spend your time, energy, and attention mindfully, ultimately increasing your effectiveness in life and work. Combined, they can make the difference between just getting by or actually getting ahead.

### Don´t Eliminate Distractions

In previous chapters we have seen what happened when you are in front of your computer, working on that project and how easily is to get distracted when you receive that email notification. Do you remember? Before you realise you have wasted more than 30 minutes in low priority task.

Open awareness isn't about minimizing the number of distractions in your life. On the contrary, it's about seeing those distractions as precisely what they are and choosing which ones deserve your attention, your focus. The essence of open awareness is observing your thoughts, senses, emotions, and tasks in a neutral way like a mental observatory. In this way, focus and awareness are closely linked.

Of course, it's not easy to change your way of thinking and looking at the world. Thankfully, there is simple process you can use to rewire your mind and it is by focusing on your distractions.

To enhance your awareness and focus we are going to use the well-known ABCD method.

This is to ensure your mind is calm, clear, and focused. Once you have developed a sufficient level of focus, you open your awareness and become an observer of your own experiences.

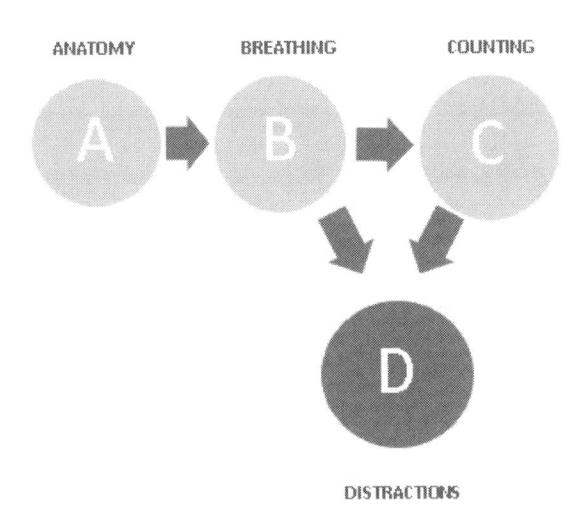

```
ANATOMY      BREATHING      COUNTING
   A      →      B      →      C
                  ↓      ↓
                    D
                DISTRACTIONS
```

**Mindfulness At Work Quick Start- Enhance Focus and Awareness**

In Mindfulness there is a technique known as the ABCD method. Follow these steps and look at the graph above to remember the steps.

The ABCD stands for Attitude, Body, Breath, Counting, Distraction.

**The Body**:
- Start by sitting comfortably

**The Breath**:

- Start by noticing the breath where it is most noticeable. It can be useful to imagine that you are watching the breath through a glass unable to change or influence it. Check off one by one whether your mind has the three core qualities of relaxation, focus, and clarity.

- When you've reached some level of these qualities, you can begin to open your awareness.

**Counting**:

- Counting is to further stabilise the breath focus; you add the number at the end of the out breath. For example, for a 10-minute session you can count down from 25. If you are doing it while working, while talking to someone over the phone, you can count while you breathe in and breath out.

- Use whatever suits you. Whatever you can incorporate into your routine.

**Distractions**:

- Let go of the attention on your breathing

- Stay aware and when you notice the first distraction (a sound, thought, physical sensation, or anything else) direct your full attention to it and use it as an anchor for your awareness.

- Just observe and don't try to do anything. Label t as you wish. 'Distraction' 'Thoughts' 'Shopping'. Simply observe it

- Focus on the distraction and when it changes or disappears, stay open for the new one. It is like surfing. You are just waiting for the next wave to stay fully focused.
- If at any point you find you're confused or overwhelmed or distracted away from distractions ;) at any time you can come back to your beathing.

While the instructions are simple, and the technique quite simple, that you can do it from your desk, the challenge for many is observing thoughts, feelings, sensations, and emotions neutrally without engaging.

Don't judge yourself. Don't expect any results. Just experience and start creating habits step by step.

In short, the space you gain when you enhance your awareness can change how you experience the world and respond to everything in life.

Remember, the objective is not to sit without distractions. The objective is to be aware of the fact that you're distracted and to acknowledge that you have the ability to regain your focus on your breath.

While training this, you are turbocharging your neural networks for when you go to work. You are training your mind to be more focused on the task at hand regardless of what it is, and at the same time to be aware when you are distracted and redirecting your focus back to the chosen task. These two skills are extremely useful in any fast paced, demanding work environment.

The ability to observe your thoughts and experiences instead of being your thoughts and experiences not only results in more effectiveness and mental peace but also preserves your energy. After all, thinking too much is the core cause of mental exhaustion.

Use this simple technique for the next week and see what you notice.

# WORK TECHNIQUES

> Much of spiritual life is self-acceptance, maybe all of it.
>
> Jack Kornfield

## Why Do We Need Mindfulness At Work?

The World Health Organization predicts work related stress, burnout, and depression to be among the world's most prevalent diseases by 2020, joining perpetual killers like stroke and diabetes.

One study by American Online found that the average person actively works there days a week.

When we are working, 49 % of our time we spend it in low priority activities.

And few different studies show that executives feel somewhere between 25 percent and 50 percent of time spent in meetings to be wasted.

Another report shows that 60 % of the people check their email on vacations, quite a good amount in the toilet, at their children's functions and even at a funeral.

At a minimum, we have a challenge.

We are holistic beings. And I am sharing some numbers to create awareness of the need to introduce Mindfulness At Work, but most probably the same happens in your personal life.

If you have children, can you relate to this lack of focus and continuous distractions?

With the rise of the Internet and the growth of mobile devices, how and where we work has shifted. We no longer need to go to work. Work comes to us. Even if we do go into the office every day, work-based problems can find us night or day, in a restaurant or at the ballpark.

Today's information-driven work environment is frequently hectic and often ambiguous, with the lines between work and home becoming more and more blurred by each new productivity app.

Thankfully, there are things we can do to better manage the challenges of today's work life to create that mental space between us and the demands and responsibilities of our information existence.

Now that we understand how our mind works, how to enhance focus and awareness, let's bring Mindfulness At Work and see how it can help you manage your most common day to day activities.

> Don't believe everything you think.
> Thoughts are just that – thoughts.
>
> Allan Lokos

## Your Area Of Control

We have seen that change is here to stay.

Some changes have been decided by you, and some others, the ones that probably frustrate you most, by others.

Acceptance is the ability to refrain from making an already difficult situation more difficult.

If you can solve the problem, why worry? Likewise, if you can't solve the problem, why worry?

A good framework for looking at this is to consider what is in your circle of control versus what is in your circle of concern.

If there is a problem that you can do something about, then you should act as if it is within your circle of control. If there is a problem that you really cannot do anything about, don't make it worse by fighting it.

A situation is as it is.

Accept it and move on, without carrying on an inner battle.

### *Your Area Of Control Is Power*

Acceptance and focusing on your area of control is a powerful way to increase your effectiveness not to mention your happiness just by changing the way you perceive obstacles and challenges.

Acceptance doesn't equate to giving up or being apathetic. It's not passivity. By all means, if you can do something to improve or change your situation, do it. If you can't change the situation, however, then why waste mental resources trying to think up a way to alter the unavoidable or inevitable?

Focusing on your area of control means to save energy to actually focus on what you can influence, change and control.

How can you tell the difference between a situation where you should keep fighting to make a change versus letting go and accepting the situation as it is?

The key is to remember that acceptance as a mental strategy is not necessarily about what you do or what you don't do; rather, it is about how you experience and perceive the world around you. I can accept that I may not be able to eliminate global warming in my lifetime, but it doesn't mean I won't continue to try and work on the things I can do. Quite the opposite. It means that I won't frustrate about what I can´t do and I will focus all my energy on what I can do.

We have the freedom to influence many things in our lives. But some things simply can't be changed. With acceptance, we cease to make difficult situations

## *Mindfulness At Work Quick Start - Your Area Of Control*

- Download the tool in Mindfulness At Work Program

- The next time you confront a situation at work, use the tool, or simply take a piece of paper. Draw two columns, one name it area of control and the other one area of concern. Vent and brainstorm about the things are under your area of concern and what are under your area of control and you will see the relief and the clarity you gain.

- Area of concern: things that you worry about, but you have no control over (weather, politics, COVID-19, reorg…)

- Area of control: things you can influence by your actions. For example, most probably you can't control that your company is going through reorg, but you can prepare yourself to embrace change, and if needed, for example, update your CV, and get better prepared in case you need to look for another job. Reorganisation is going to happen whether you like it or not. So, don't waste your time and energy thinking on that but instead focusing on the things you can actually influence.

- This simple but powerful technique gives you the freedom and encouragement to act and influence your future.

- I encourage you to use it in your team meetings as well. Sometimes we get lost in focusing on the area of concern when we should be focusing on things we can do to influence. What can I do for?

> Open the window of your mind. Allow the fresh air, new lights and new truths to enter.
>
> Amit Ray

## Mindful Emails

How many emails do you receive every day?

How many of them are actually helpful or require your intervention?

I won't write about WhatsApp or IMs but same applies. We make a terrible use of emails and digital communication in general.

Many people use email as one-way street for communication and to cover themselves instead of the main purpose of email communication, that is, collaboration.

Recent studies show the aver-age person sends and receives around 100 e-mails a day.

Regardless of your job, your location, or your industry, e-mail probably takes up a significant portion of your time at work- and life- and represent one of your main distractions.

This is the reason it is the first work technique, so you can see the benefits of Mindfulness At Work from day one.

### *Email and Dopamine (yes, it is back!)*

As mentioned earlier, one report shows 60 percent of Americans check their e-mail on vacation, and 25 percent become restless and unwell after just three days without access to e-mail. In fact, doctors have estimated 11 million Americans suffer from "e-mail addiction.

When you receive a compliment, and interesting email that requires your action or if you reply can show off how knowledgeable you are, your brain releases dopamine the neurotransmitter that makes you feel good. And as we have seen before, it is like a sugar high. It creates addition. Your brain wants more of it.

Mindfulness practice helps create awareness of your thoughts, feelings, and cravings.

You have a choice in avoiding e-mail addiction. The first is to eliminate all notifications.

### *Turn Off All Your Digital Notifications*

Turn off not only email notification but also WhatsApp, IM…

I know it really depends on the nature of your work, but for most people we don't need to look at every email, IM or WhatsApp the second we receive it. If it is urgent, they should call you. But that is a culture you need to introduce in your organisation, with your team.

Try working for a couple days with the notifications switched off. After that, you can make an informed decision about what works best for you.

### *Micro-blocking Time*

If you have read my book ScrewProcrastinationTakeAction, you are familiar with this technique.

Many people leave their e-mail open all day long.

If you allow your focus to shift every time a new e-mail arrives, you're wasting time. It takes your brain several seconds to concentrate on a new e-mail, and then the same time again to return your focus to your previous work or perhaps even longer. Shifting back and forth between tasks uses up a lot of energy, making you less effective overall.

For most people, it brings them down toward the distracted and autopilot end of The Matrix of Mental Effectiveness.

Allocate only certain, fixed times during the day to fully focus on e-mail.

When should you deal with your e-mail?

This depends on your job and your organization's culture (though here most probably you can influence and change it following the tips for Mindfulness At Work Quick Start below). One e-mail session in the morning (not first thing) and one again just before or after lunch is ideal. I also recommend checking 30 minutes before your end your shift in case you need to take action on anything urgent. It will help you plan your priorities for following day so you can disconnect and rest before you turn off your screen.

### **Turn Off Your Screen 60 minutes At the Beginning and At The End of Your Day**

Opening your e-mail first thing in the morning immediately takes you to react to someone else's agenda and short-term problems

In the first half of the morning, the brain is generally most alert, most focused, and most creative.

Your early morning creative energy dissipates, and you wasted opportunity to use your mind at its highest potential. Ideally you want to use that energy and creativity to focus on things that matter most, on your important goals and decide the priorities for your day.

Try waiting at least half an hour to an hour after you get to work before checking your inbox and switch off all your devices at least 60 minutes before going to sleep.

Remember that mindfulness at work can help to enhance focus and get better results doing less. Less of what is not important and more and better of what matters most for you and your business.

You can try to put email sessions on your calendar as fixed activities, with the rest of your activities planned around them.

**Emotions and E-Mail**

When the mind receives too little information about a sender's intentions, it composes its own story. Individuals are often convinced a self-created story is true. To make matters worse, the mind has a tendency to emphasize negative stories over positive ones. In other words, we tend to assume the worst. But why?

The reason that we struggle with effective electronic communication is simply that words are not the primary way we internalize messages. In fact, research has shown that 60 percent of communication is understood through body language, and another 33 percent through tone of voice.

That leaves only 7 percent for the actual. Since e-mail only uses 7 percent of your communication potential, there's an enormously high probability for misunderstanding. In this sense, autopilot can be your worst enemy. Improving your awareness can make you far less likely to create misunderstanding, worry, and conflict.

Avoiding emotional e-mailing means being aware of your own thought patterns: it means being aware of the stories your mind creates before you end up believing them or making them worse...

Before you start reading e-mails, take a few moments to relax. When you come across an e-mail that generates negative reactions, stop. Do not give in to the impulse to answer immediately. Instead, start by thinking calmly about how the e-mail makes you feel: defensive? angry? sad?

An impulsive answer can easily cause more harm than good. I talk from experience!

With the years I learn it the hard way. Most of the times driven by my values. And it did more harm that anything.

Mindfulness doesn't say do not send this email. Instead, it encourages you to create the space

Take the time to think about what kind of response will have the most beneficial outcome, both for you and the sender.

Maybe the best response isn't an e-mail at all, but a quick call to air out an issue or clear up any misunderstanding.

When it comes to mindful e-mail here some tips and protocols that can help:

**Mindfulness At Work Quick Start-Emails**

Awareness:

- Take a moment to reflect on your use of e-mail and your relationship with your inbox.
- Is e-mail a source of distraction for you?

Creating the space. Ask yourself:

- Should this e-mail be sent at all? And should all these people be copied
- Does the e-mail contain the information needed for it to be understood correctly?
- How will the recipient perceive this e-mail? Put yourself in the recipient's shoes.
- Sometimes it helps to write and email, with an empty TO line (be careful!) or sent it to yourself, and vent as much as you want. Put it to sleep and read it the following morning with a calm and focus mind.

Give the importance on email on our day to day, I have sharing these extra tips:

**Top 25 email protocols**

1. Keep it short. Before you hit Send, look through your email and eliminate everything that doesn't add to your desired outcome.

2. Make an actionable subject line. A good subject line is like a good headline—it makes people want to read the rest. If you're sending an email asking someone to do something, put that into your subject line. Example: "Review Budget Documents."

3. Avoid vague one-word subject lines. No one wants to read an email lazily titled "Stuff" Be on target as to what the email contains. This also helps to keep the body of your message concise.

4. Don't discuss more than one subject. It's called the subject line, not the subjects' line. If you have to address more than one topic send more than one email. Following this practice makes communication easier and helps eliminate lengthy messages

5. Don't rely on the high-priority indicator (such as "!" or "!!"). What is important to you usually isn't important to others. Sad but true. Use a compelling subject line instead.

6. Write the body of the email first, before filling in the "To:" line. We almost instinctively enter the recipient first thing. Try to retrain your brain to have this be the last thing you do. Most people have embarrassed themselves at least once by accidentally sending a message before it was finished. Don't let hitting Send when you meant to hit Attach or Save cost you your career!

7. List the action steps first. People tend to read only the first paragraph anyway, even if you have vital information, so don't bury the point of your message at the end.

8. Be clear about who you're asking to take the actions. If the message is addressed more than one person (including ccs) and requests action, list what you are asking each recipient to do. Be specific. Include by when.

9. If the message is short, put it in the subject line and put (EOM) at the end. This stands for "end of message." Using it let's the recipients know they don't need to open the message.

You'll be saving everyone time. Example: "The meeting is starting in 15 minutes (EOM)."

10. Put (NRN) at the end of your message. This means "no reply needed." Of course, only use this when applicable. People will be silently thanking you.

11. Use prefixes when necessary. Writing "Q1" lets people know the urgency of the email and they'll know exactly how they need to respond. But don't cry wolf. Only use Q1 if it really is urgent and important. And if that's the case, is email really the best way to communicate? This brings us to our next point...

12. Don't rely on email for Q1 matters. Yes, emails are sent within a matter of seconds, but that doesn't guarantee they'll be read within seconds. Don't forget that telephones can still be used to talk directly to one another. Or maybe just getting out of your chair and walking across the hall to have a conversation would be more helpful.

13. Avoid using too many acronyms. Acronyms are great time savers, especially if included in the subject line. But thousands exist, which makes it less likely your reader will know what you're talking about. However, some

communication can establish a few common uses in your office. Examples: AR (action required), FYA (for your approval), or QUE (question).

14. Respond within twenty-four hours. Of course, this depends on the nature of the email. If it's a Q2 problem that can be addressed later in the week, at least send a message informing the sender when to expect a response.

15. Don't expect an immediate response. Since we've advised people to only check their emails at certain parts of their scheduled day, you should be doing the same. So only expect a response within a reasonable amount of time.

16. Use out-of-office replies. When you are going to be out for an extended period of time, let people know. You can usually set out-of-office replies for people in your organization, people outside the organization, or both. Some programs let you restrict these replies to people on your contacts list. This is good, because it prevents automatic replies to spam engines, which can increase the amount of spam you receive.

17. Eliminate unnecessary ccs. People overuse the cc function daily. Make sure you are only cc'ing people who need to be ccd. Note that, usually, a cc implies no action is required, but that you are just sharing information. If you want someone in the cc line to take action, make sure to spell it out.

18. Use bcc very, very carefully. This is best used when your recipients do not know one another. That way you don't give out anyone's contact information. And some smartphones today may not necessarily show that you were

bcc'd, leaving you wide open to reply when you were not seen as one of the recipients. Not good.

19. Don't use reply all. You know how low value most reply all are ... stay out of that camp. We thank you, and others will too!

20. Label your attachments appropriately. Don't leave recipients guessing which file is which by labelling attachments "document 1.docx" or "CB0056.pdf opt for clearer titles.
Example: "Minutes From 5/6 Retooling Meeting."

21. Summarize discussion threads. If you're forwarding a discussion to another person, it's useful to summarize the discussion rather than having him or her scroll through the entire thing. Or you can highlight only the relevant parts of your message.

22. Always add new contacts to your address book. This avoids the risk of a future email getting sent to your junk folder.

23. Make sure your signature includes contact information. This helps if someone needs to contact you immediately or wishes to talk specifics with you through another form of communication.

24. Don't send emails for private matters. Work email is not private and is considered company property. Save personal matters for your breaks. Plus, why clutter your valuable email space with personal messages better suited for another account?

25. Don't use email unless you have to. Lots of us can get over one hundred messages per day. If you can simply walk down the hall to a co-worker's office, do that. Or if the email takes you more than ten minutes to type, it may be too long for this mode of communication. In general, email works best when used to give and receive information. It is less effective (or even counterproductive) when used to solve conflict, vent, voice strong opinions, gossip, reprimand, or complain. There are better ways to communicate these things ...or, for some, maybe it's better not to communicate them at all.

> A few simple tips for life: feet on the ground, head to the skies, heart open…quiet mind.
>
> Rasheed Ogunlaru

# Mindful Meetings

Quite often people find meetings to be a waste of time. Which make things worse when we research show that leaders think that between 25 percent and 50 percent of time spent in meetings to be wasted.

And it gets worse. Research shows we are only productive 50 % of our time and the rest of the time is taken up by unproductive activities like inefficient or unnecessary meetings.

Meetings are supposed to allow us to benefit from collective wisdom and experience, ideally allowing us to accomplish things we couldn't otherwise do on our own.

This technique looks at ways we can use mindfulness as an effective tool to get the most out of meetings.

### *Mindfulness At Work Quick Start for Mindful Meetings*

During the next few weeks to implement mindful meetings, start by considering one simple question: are your meetings for your benefit and the benefit of others?

If the answer is "yes," then the most important is making meetings more effective for yourself and for others.

Reflect for a moment on meetings in your work environment.It is good to ask for feedback as well.

A best practice would be to do an EBI (even better if exercise) with your team to reflect on your meeting culture.

- How effective are they?
- What is not working?
- What can you do to help make better use of them?

Once you have reviewed your meeting culture and have decided to continue with the meeting, follow these steps.

**1-Before the meeting**

Shifting your focus onto three things:

- The people you're with
- The meeting agenda
- And yourself

Here's what to do: before you enter the meeting room, direct full attention to your breath, letting each and every internal and external distractions go.

While doing your own mental preparation can be beneficial, preparing as a group can help improve the mental effectiveness of everyone in attendance. You don't even need to call it mindfulness. Before you introduce an agenda, simply invite meeting participants to take a brief mental break, to relax, settle their mind, and become present in the room.

## 2-The meeting

A clear purpose, a defined agenda, agreeing on timing, managing tangents, and adhering to timelines are all solid guidelines for conducting effective meetings. Even with all of these standards in place, a meeting is only effective if everyone is paying attention. If participants have their laptops open or phones in hand, the collective mental capacity that should be the hallmark of successful meetings simply isn't there.

In meetings, presence forms the foundation for effectiveness.

The fundamental rule for a mindful meeting is be completely present with those you are together with for as long as you are all together.

Every meeting you're in, you have the opportunity to make the people you're with the anchor of your attention. To do so, focus your attention as long as you are all together.

Certainly, there are times when computers and phones are important during a meeting. But before turning them on, ensure their use is tied to helping enhance the meeting instead of simply acting as a convenient distraction. Similarly, when your phone buzzes, pause for a second. Think about your priorities and

goals.

- Do I have an agenda?
- Do we have an agreed time?
- Do we have clear speakers?

- Are Laptops/phones necessary?
- Who is the Minute Taker?
- Who is the Timekeeper?

**3-Wrap Up**

Concluding meetings at the right time and in the right way can be an art. It's important to be mindful of ending meetings on time so that everyone can move on to their next activity. As a meeting up wraps, be sure any "action items," "follow-ups," or "next steps" are clearly documented and assigned.

Also, if the meeting finishes at an appropriate time, there's less of a rush. This means you have the opportunity to look coworkers in the eye and thank them for their time and attention. When a meeting is concluded with gratitude and appreciation, people are more willing to meet again and a positive pattern for meetings develops.

Review Actions items.

- What?
- Who/
- By When?
- Thank the attention


Meetings can be a powerful way of collaboration and creativity but only if managed correctly.

Move away from the idea that meetings or 121 are necessary. Only the are if you have a purpose and you are present. If any of these two are missing, you are wasting your time.

> How you look at it is pretty much
>
> how you'll see it.
>
> Rasheed Ogunlaru

## Mindful Goals

Like a GPS, our goals show us the way, even when there is traffic, if we have a clear goal, the GPS will show us the different ways to get to our destination.

And we all have goals. Whether they are personal or professional, whether we are consciously aware or not, we all have goals.

Mindfulness and goals go well together. In fact, successfully achieving one is hard without the other. When you have clear goals, it's far easier to stay focused and aware. Similarly, when you're focused and aware, it's easier to keep your actions aligned with your goals.

Of course, achieving goals isn't always easy. Many obstacles can get in the way. This technique presents mindful approaches to reaching your goals. But before diving into the criteria for mindful goal setting, let's examine how our subconscious can prevent you from achieving goals.

### *New Year Resolutions Do Not Work*

If you read my book ScrewProcrastinationTakeacions you know that New years' resolution do not work.

They don't work if you don't do them mindfully.

How many times have you made a New Year's resolution? Only to realize twelve months later that you are in the same situation.

We start the year full on motivation but usually in February, the motivation declines until it completely disappears.

Why? What goes wrong? To answer that question, we need to understand a bit more about how our mind works.

Our mind operates simultaneously on conscious and subconscious levels. Many of our subconscious processes are rooted in the reptilian and limbic parts of our brain—the foundations for our survival instincts and the centre of our emotions. Our conscious processes like language, problem solving, and creativity, operate mainly in our cortex.

While our brain can consciously process around seven bits, or pieces, of information per second, it's nothing compared to the 11 million bits our subconscious handles in the same amount of time. This means there's much more happening beneath the surface of our conscious mind than we're aware of.

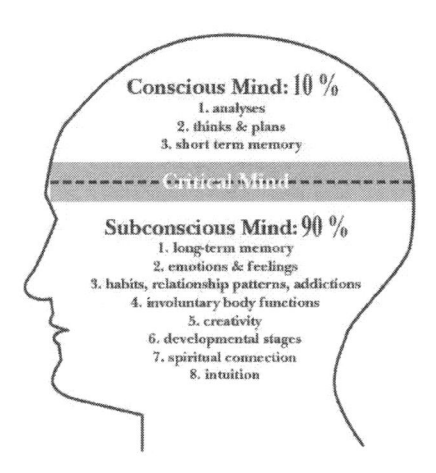

**Conscious Mind:** 10 %
1. analyses
2. thinks & plans
3. short term memory

------- Critical Mind -------

**Subconscious Mind:** 90 %
1. long-term memory
2. emotions & feelings
3. habits, relationship patterns, addictions
4. involuntary body functions
5. creativity
6. developmental stages
7. spiritual connection
8. intuition

Our conscious mind takes 10 % of our decisions and our subconscious can take up to 90 % of our decisions.

When you make a New Year's resolution, you make it consciously. With your analytical part of your brain. And while you might think that the seven bits per second your conscious mind can handle should be enough to follow through and achieve the goal, the reality is that in daily life you're constantly bombarded with distractions that require conscious attention. Many great resolutions can get drowned in this sea of distractions.

Your subconscious may be another barrier to achieving your goals. While your New Year's resolution makes sense for your conscious mind, subconscious processes may take you in another direction. And your subconscious mind is driving you 90 % of the time.

So, when it comes to maintaining clear goals, it's important to collaborate with both our conscious and subconscious mind. Our subconscious is primarily driven by two simple motivations: grasping for things we like and avoiding things we don't like. While our subconscious often craves short-term gratification because it is driven by emotions, our conscious goals more often include delayed gratification.

It is said that our conscious mind sets the goals, and our subconscious mind achieves them.

And there are three main reasons. One is the extremely power of the subconscious brain of 11 million bits, the second is that 90 % of our time our decision are taken by the subconscious and third is that if a goal motivates me, my actions are driven by my emotions which at the same time drive 90 % of my actions.

That is why is very important that you set up goals in a way that motivate you, your team and your find the WIIFM (what is it for me)

Mindfulness allows you to better align your conscious goals with your subconscious processes, keeping your goals center stage and enhancing your chances of success.

The way you set goals can play a big role in your ability to achieve them.

Two simple techniques can help you more effectively communicate goals to your subconscious:

### *Mindful SMART-D-Goal Setting*

Clearly defined and specific goals are easier for your subconscious to understand. While the subconscious has amazing processing power, it's not the most organized.

By default, the subconscious moves toward the desirable and away from the unpleasant. Whereas a negatively framed goal might be I want to avoid multitasking, the positive version is I want to focus on one task at a time. With the second framing, you're clearly moving toward something positive—and the processing power of your subconscious mind can help you get there.

In Seven Habits of Highly Effective People, Steven Covey asked, "What is the point of reaching the top of the ladder, to find that it was against the wrong wall?"

Goals are important—and often hard to achieve. With a mind that's focused and clear, setting and reaching our goals becomes much easier, as does letting go of those goals that may turn out to be detrimental to our happiness.

**Mindfulness At Work Quick Start - Mindful Goals**

- Take a moment to write down your key goals for professional life and for your personal life. Make them specific and positively framed to increase your potential for success.

- Follow the well-known guidelines of a SMART Goal. I always add -D- at the end. Discomfort. If you want to achieve something different, your actions need to be different. Get out of your comfort zone or you will achieve same results.

- I change SMART to SMART-D-
    - Specific
    - Motivation
    - Achievable (but remember the D)

- Relevant (and ecologic meaning that they should be aligned with other areas of your life)

- Time-bound. Always in present tense, like it has already happened and with a maximum date on it. The reason for this is that your subconscious mind, the one that will help achieve your goals, will always look at the easiest and quicker way of achieving your goals. For example: It is maximum 30th March and I have published the Spanish edition of Mindfulness At work.

- D-Discomfort. The magic starts outside of your comfort zone.

Use the SMART-D- template and the wheel of roles in Mindfulness At Work Program and make this year your best year ever.

Nothing can harm you as much as your own thoughts unguarded.

Buddha

## Mindful Priorities

As we have seen we all have personal and professional goals. Same as with focus and awareness, goals, and priorities they need to go together.

To be successful, we need to have clear goals and at the same time to be able to prioritize which goals are most important.

There is a reality. Goals will conflict.

Mindfulness can help us declutter our minds and focus on fewer things. With greater awareness, we can ensure we're turning our attention toward the right goals: our most important goals.

A common management framework, the 80/20 principle—also known as the Pareto principle-proposes that 80 percent of our time and effort goes into activities that only generate 20 percent of outcomes. This means we spend the majority of our time on activities that produce a proportionally small amount of results.

Ideally, instead we should focus on activities that generate that other 80 percent of our desired outcomes.

When we're more focused and aware, we spend our time on the activities that generate the greatest return for the least effort.

When we're distracted, when we're on autopilot, it's easy to do lot of "busywork" that takes a lot of time but delivers few results.

Being busy doesn't necessarily equate to being effective. Sound familiar?

Franklin Covey Institute looked at the workplace activities of over 350,000 people. What they found was that most people spend an average of 41 percent on low-priority activities as opposed to priorities that are truly pressing.

When the mind's under pressure—when it never gets a break from being bombarded with information and distractions it can be difficult to maintain focus, let alone prioritize tasks.

In many ways, we're actually addicted to the action itself. When we are confused, we feel the need to accomplish something, even if it is a small task even if it is not aligned with our goals. In the middle of that confusion some people feel they need to show themselves -and to their boss or colleagues – that they are busy.

Can you think of someone that always, no matter what happens, will tell you how busy he/she is?

The most important is noy how busy you are but if you are focusing on the right important goals.

### *Much busyness is created by our action addiction*

When we're under pressure, we tend to rush toward instant gratification—the things we can control or accomplish right this second.

When we're addicted to action, we do things not because they're important, but because we want to feel important. The tasks are in front of us, and we want to be useful and productive. The problem is, when we don't step back to ensure we're spending time on tasks aligned with our main goals, we end up wasting a lot of time on immediate though often inessential tasks.

Action addiction is one of the biggest threats to our mental effectiveness and productivity.

Action addiction takes away your ability to maintain clear priorities and work toward your most important goals. But by now you know that you have a neurotransmitter -called serotonin produced in the brain during mindfulness practice- that balances the dopamine that kick action addiction creates.

What should you do when you experience conflicting priorities?

### *Freedom of Choice*

The main cause of action addition is conflicting. When two or more priorities conflict, you reach a choice point: a point at which you need to decide how to best manage multiple priorities and what step are you going to take next.

When we are not clear about our priorities, we just jump into action looking for the dopamine high.

But, as you now know, not all action is aligned with our goals.

When priorities conflict, take a breath before you jump into action.

Some people may say, "If I have to take a conscious breath every priorities conflict, it'll take me all day to get anything done." The solution to this problem is to learn how to speed up by slowing down.

**Mindfulness At Work Quick Start to Mindful Priorities**

- For the next week, when you arrive at your desk, just as you are about to get started, sit down, and look out the window or into your blank computer screen.

- <u>Don't act. Don't talk. Don't solve a problem. Don´t open you email or your smartphone.</u>

- Just sit and think about your priorities for the day.

- Think how they align to your important goals.

- And choose the top three for the day. The ones that will get you closer to your goals.

- When you have a conflict priority, breath and recall your priorities and then make a decision based on your overarching goals. You have the freedom of choice. You choose your next step.

- By taking a brief pause, you're able to maintain your focus and awareness. But we usually don't do it because we are going like headless chicken.

- These steps allow you to respond to situations with the most appropriate action—to concentrate on your priorities and goals—rather than simply acting on autopilot.
- Do this for the rest of the week and see how you feel

Nothing is forever except change.

Buddha

# Mindful Planning

Same as with goals and priorities, whether we realize it or not, we make plans in our life and work intentionally and involuntarily.

Planning goes hand in hand with priorities. Mindful planning requires clarity of priorities, move away from a headless chicken approach, and invest your time in Q2.

As you can see the matrix of mental effectiveness is aligned with the urgent-important matrix.

We should spend most of our time in Q2.

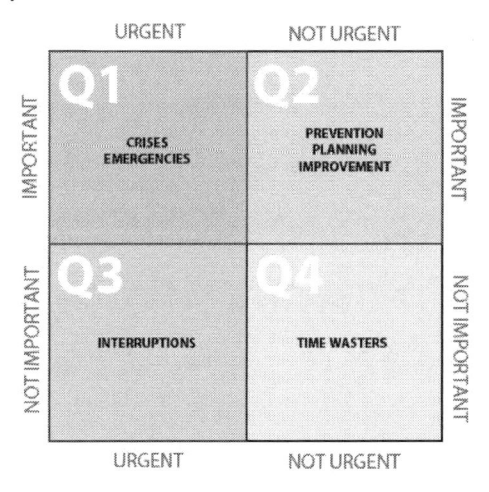

|  | URGENT | NOT URGENT |
|---|---|---|
| **IMPORTANT** | Q1 — CRISES, EMERGENCIES | Q2 — PREVENTION, PLANNING, IMPROVEMENT |
| **NOT IMPORTANT** | Q3 — INTERRUPTIONS | Q4 — TIME WASTERS |

It is the quadrant of extraordinary productivity and mindfulness.

I talk quite a lot about it in my book ScrewProcrastinationTakeAction that goes with the Action Planning.

It is important to plan but it has to be mindful planning accompanied with mindful actions or otherwise you will go on the opposite direction.

The reality is that our mind wants to plan even when we try to sleep. Instead of being focused on an important conversation, our mind starts planning what we'll have for lunch.

While mindful planning is both built on our experiences from the past and directed toward the future, it's always done in the present moment.

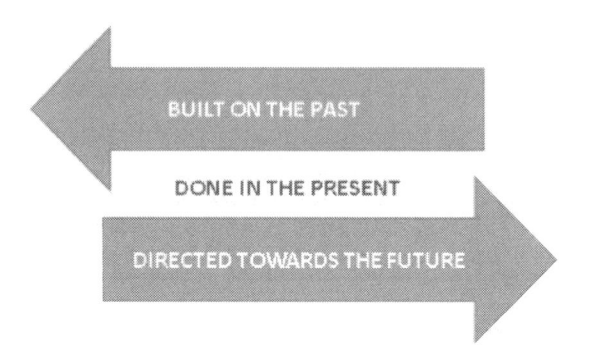

BUILT ON THE PAST

DONE IN THE PRESENT

DIRECTED TOWARDS THE FUTURE

**"The bad news is, time flies: the good news is, you're the pilot."**

Conducting clear planning every day can help each and every one of us become better pilots.

It will also make us more mindful.

Clear planning makes it easier for you to live a more mindful life, and mindfulness, in turn, helps you plan more clearly. In this sense, clear planning and mindfulness are complementary, both helping to keep you in quadrant 2 of the matrix of mental effectiveness and extraordinary productivity.

Being present in the moment doesn't require a change in the actual things you do or the way you live your life; rather, it's a change in how you pay attention. Being present in the moment is a conscious decision.

In order to make mindful planning it is important that you make time to plan.

Time flies especially fast when we feel like we lack control. And we're not in control if we suffer from action addiction. When compelled by any addiction, we're not free to think clearly or act rationally.

We are driven not by choice, but by the urge. With the rush of dopamine.

The morning is the most important choice point of the day. As it sets the tone for the rest of the day, it's critical to begin the morning with a period of clear planning.

When you take the time to plan your day, you gain peace and quiet by knowing that time has been reserved for major priorities.

It's a small investment with a big return.

Slowing down can be an effective way of speeding up. Starting the day with focus and clarity allows you to work more effectively than simply following each and every distraction that arises.

Putting effort into clear planning keeps your co-workers or other distractions from hijacking your time.

Mindful planning has applications beyond just organizing your day. Weekly and monthly planning sessions can help you keep the big picture in mind and manage your calendar accordingly.

See my book and agenda ScrewProcrastinationTakeAction for more details. You can also request the downloadable tools. See appendix.

**Mindful Scheduling**

The most important is to allocate most of your time to completing activities that deliver the greatest outcomes for the least amount of effort following the 80/20 rule while still leaving time for the urgent matters that will inevitably crop up. Whatever you decide, saving a realistic margin of unscheduled time can help you avoid being put under unnecessary pressure.

Also consider how much time your mental batteries every day—whether through small breaks, a short walk, or your time for some mindfulness practice.

It is also important to reserve time for unavoidable "transition" activities, such as commuting, rest between meetings...etc

Just as clear planning can help you reach your professional goals, it can do the same in your personal life. Think about dedicating quality, one-on-one time with your child or setting aside an evening with your partner or a close friend. Think about the kinds of activities you need to do for yourself to stay happy and healthy.

Most of the people do not block time in the calendar for ´´personal´ meetings. Meetings with themselves- ME time- or meetings/activities with their love ones. And these are your most important meetings in live.

Personally, I go to a mindfulness retreat at least once a year because I know it's crucial to my ability to help others find calm and realize their potential. If you don't dedicate time to reflecting on your goals and priorities, time will fly by on autopilot. You'll feel out of control, with precious moments slipping away. But by mindfully planning, you'll achieve greater success at work and at home.

You'll use each moment well.

Which is good because it won't come again. You are only live once.

### *Mindfulness At Work Quick Start for Mindful Planning*

- Consider the implement the 30/10 rule that it is on your Mindfulness At Work Programme

- Assign every week, the last day of the week, 30 minutes to review the current week and plan the following week. That way your head with rest and you will plan mindfully.

- Each day assign 10 minutes at the beginning of the day to review your priorities and choose your top three. Also take the following into account:

- Allocate time for preparation

- Determining how much time you should leave free for urgent matters

- Plan time for recharging your batteries

- Plan your lunch (this one and previous one highly important if you are working from home)

- Planning for transition activities, such as meeting follow-up and travel.

- Now, get to work. Review your plan once or twice during the day to track your progress.

- At the end of the day, allocate 10 minutes to review your day and plan tomorrow.

Be where you are, otherwise, you will miss your life.

Buddha

## Mindful Communication

Sending a message is not the same as communicating a message. For effective communication to occur, the receiver must understand what the sender intended—not just hear or read the words.

The foundation of mindful communication is, as in many other aspects of life, being fully present in interactions with other people. Only when we're fully present, we can be sure to understand what's actually being communicated.

Empathy plays an important role in communication.

If you have a sense of how the person with whom you're trying to communicate feels, it's easier to connect.

Empathy and emotional Intelligence play an important role in in mindful communication

Generally speaking, we have two challenges to overcome. The first one is that our mind has a tendency to wander and the second one is our tendency of our mind's orientation to see things as we expect to see them, commonly known as habitual perception.

Habitual perception, or cognitive rigidity as it's also known is the mind's natural desire to place reality into simple, pre-existing categories. Both our wandering minds and this rigidity affects our communication skills.

**Be Honest. Are You Mindfully Listening?**

We all have minds that wander. We all get trapped by our habitual perceptions. We've all had the experience of assuming we know what someone will say before they say it. But making that assumption can undercut communication before it even has a chance to begin.

Mindful communication is based on avoiding both a wandering mind and your habitual perception.

If we refer back to the matrix, in quadrant two we find the key ingredients to effective communication: attention, empathy, understanding are all present.

Awareness of the factors that influence what we listen for and who we listen to can empower us to change our listening habits. We can listen verbally, nonverbally, and relationally, using *all five senses*. We listen relationally by reading between the lines based on what we know about the relationship and our conversation partner from past experiences. When we do this, we can experience higher quality conversations with others. We can also build quality relationships with others and improve the relationships we are already in.

Listening mindfully requires us to comprehend what the other person is actually saying. Then we need to let them know we are paying attention and thinking about what they shared. We do this by showing interest and support through maintaining eye contact, nodding, smiling, and encouraging them to express their thoughts. In a sense, we become emotionally involved in their message and it shows.

***Mindfulness At Work Quick Start- Mindful Communication***

To communicate effectively we need to focus on listening and talking.

**Mindful Listening**

In Mindfulness we use the acronym STOP-be Silent, Tuned in, Open, and Present—to make it easy to remember:

Here's how to put STOP into practice.

- **Be Silent**. Being silent means switching off your external and internal voice.
- **Tune In.** Create a connection between your body language and your intentions. You can smile, nod…
- **Be Open**. Switch off any habitual perception you may have. Listen with your beginner mind
- **Be Present**. Be fully present as long as you're interacting with the other person. Nowadays it is a luxury to have someone full attention.

***Mindful talking***

In mindfulness we use the acronym ACT to use mindful talking: Appropriate, Compassionate, and Timed

- **Be Appropriate**. Say the right words, to the right person, at the right time. Put another way, ensure what you're saying is useful and beneficial to the other person

- **Be Compassionate**. Speak with a desire to contribute to the other person's well-being. But understand being compassionate doesn't mean keeping quiet when someone's made a mistake. In fact, providing people with constructive feedback on their actions can be very compassionate and it can help them lean, develop, and grow.
- **Be Timed**. Say what has to be said and no more. Say what needs to be said, and then stop.

Through effective communication, you can build empathy, emotional intelligence, build relationship, create teamwork, and enhance the well-being of others.

Communication is fundamental to the success of any organization. Most of the HR legal cases in a company are driven by conflict. And conflict is driven by no well-managed communication.

Much of our success at work depends on how well we're able to engage with our colleagues, employees, supervisors, customers, and suppliers, we need to both hear them and influence them, understand them and guide them.

Same in any area of our life. Can you think of a time when you were not talking mindfully? Would you do something different today?

> Looking at beauty in the world, is the first step of purifying the mind.
>
> Amit Ray

## Mindful Creativity

Change and Creativity go hand by hand.

Without creative and innovative ideas, the changes of an organisation being successful in the long term are not good. Yet, being creative and innovative is getting more and more difficult.

One of the main barriers, as we saw in previous chapter is multitasking and the autopilot.

But on the other side reality, and clients, demand high quality creative ideas by yesterday.

And there is a fact that you have probably understood now. And it is that managing attention is vital to creativity.

In other words, if your mind wanders, it's almost impossible to be creative.

One of the challenges of being creative in today's fast-paced world is not that we don't think enough. Most people think a lot.

The issue, actually, is the opposite: many people aren't able to stop thinking. They can't let go of thoughts and distractions long enough to create space for new ideas. In the 'always on' digital era it's not always easy to turn "off."

Our tendency to think about problems and issues in habitual ways is one of the main barriers to creativity. Often, we choose solutions that we're familiar with or that have already produced success.

Our typical response to most problems is to ruminate. And then ruminate some more, spinning through the same issues without generating any new or fresh ideas.

To break this natural tendency, we simply need to stop and create that space.

Just long enough to let our synapses fire and our limbic, or subconscious, brain to take over. You see, creativity comes from tapping into the potential ideas outside our limited conscious awareness.

Creative thinking, that is, the generation of creative ideas, can begin in the fourth quadrant of the matrix, but for us to be able to capture, retain, and make use of these ideas, we need to be in quadrant two. In the second quadrant, we're not only aware of when good ideas occur, but we also have the ability to hold on to them with focus so we can apply and execute them.

One of the real barriers to creativity is the fact that we're so busy. We don't feel we have enough time or energy to walk through each step in the process below.

However, it doesn't necessarily take a lot of time or major adjustments to your everyday life to cultivate creativity. With a few brief, but intentional changes, a more present, calm, and creative mind is well within your reach.

### *Mindfulness At Work Quick Start - Mindful Creativity*

**Specify the Problem:**

If you want the help of the unconscious mind you have to give it a simple and clear problem. You know it is very powerful but needs specific directions. Have a clear idea of the problem and write down the specific question you need an answer to. For example: "Who can help me to work on this project?

**Let it Go:**

If you continue focusing on the problem your conscious brain will block any subconscious activity.

Instead, take the piece of paper with your question on it and put away.

**Create Space:**

When you create space, you let the problem to sink into your subconscious while you continue with your life business as usual.

Probably you have heard that Picasso found taking a bath to be effective in letting go of mental clutter, something entirely different may work for you.

Some people find meditation, napping, exercise or walking in nature very effective. Find what relaxes you.

**Write:**

You have given time to the subconscious to work on the problem. Now you need to connect the subconscious with your conscious. Take a blank piece of paper and draw or write without trying to be specific. Just write. Give yourself time for the answer to take shape.

That's why journaling is so powerful.

If you see that you are not ready yet and the ideas or solutions do not come to your mind, go back, and create more space and time.

**Be Mindful With Yourself**

Cultivating creativity and innovation in your subconscious takes time. But the more you work at it -the more you strengthen the connection between your conscious and subconscious mind-the easier it becomes.

In general, by simplifying your life and your mind, you can strengthen your own creative flow. All of these simple adjustments can help you have a greater mental capacity for cultivating creativity and new ideas.

A full mind is like a full cup: if there's no room for anything new, new ideas will spill over the side and be wasted. Research shows that simplicity in your working life equates to better creative flow.

In this way, less truly is more.

> Fear is a natural reaction to moving closer to the truth.
>
> Pema Chödrön

## Mindful Commuting

Since March I have been working from home. And I miss it.

I miss it because I truly enjoy working in a team and visiting clients and because somehow it was my ME time.

It was my time to think, plan and read. However, sometimes it could be very stressful, especially in cities like London, not only because of the crazy traffic but in my case, instead of ME time, sometimes I ended up multitasking while commuting and by the time I got to the office or to meet the client I was already stressed out.

Probably that has happened to you as well.

You've likely arrived at work with your mind still preoccupied by what happened throughout your morning. Or maybe you've arrived home after work, but your mind didn't arrive with you: it was still working away at the office. If you've experienced either of these states, you've been on autopilot. You've been sacrificing your own productivity, effectiveness, and well-being. But most important, you've been missing out on valuable moments in your life.

Commuting with mindfulness is a simple yet profound way to reclaim this time and spend it in a worthwhile way: on cultivating greater focus and clarity.

The minutes or hours we use commuting to and from work are valuable. Rather than letting them go to waste on the frustrations of freeway congestion or the illusion of multitasking, use them to develop focus and clarity. Allow yourself to take a well-earned break from your thoughts. Enjoy the experience of driving, riding, or sitting.

Effectively used, commuting time can ensure we arrive at work with clarity and at home with full presence. By separating work and home with a mindful commute, we have the potential to enhance work life balance.

With this technique you really feel the ´space´ that allows you to choose your next mindful step.

### *Mindfulness At Work Quick Start for Mindful Commuting*

There are a few specific instructions for commuting with mindfulness, depending on how you travel.

Here some ideas.

**Public transport:** if you are not actively driving you can use any of the breathing or focus methods that we have covered. It could be the perfect time to introduce some techniques while commuting.

**Driving:** If you're are driving, you can listen to relax music, focus on your breathing or even in your driving. Anything can be a good anchor to enhance focus.

**Longer journeys:** My favourite one. What a luxury is to be on a long-haul flight with no mail and phone calls.

Unfortunately, digital ere has also ruined these quiet times while flying. Wi-Fi onboard!

During these long journeys mindfulness can be a great way to arrive refreshed and restored. Take as long as you want to do some breathing exercises, stay present, declutter and enjoy the present.

Change the label of commuting to whatever motivates you.ME time, mindfulness, reading time, podcast time…whatever nurtures you.

An average person commutes two hours a day in some busy cities like London. If you multiply that for, let's say 20 years of commuting that gives you 10,400 hrs which is almost a year and a half of your life.

What could you do with a year and a half if you switch to mindful commuting? Study? Listening to your favourite podcast? Learn languages? Just Be?

> You are the sky. Everything else is just the weather.
>
> Pema Chödrön

## Mindful Breaks

This is an important technique to keep your energy levels and focus up.

Many of us are working from home now. We are busy, we forget to take a break. It is difficult to separate work life from your personal life. It is difficult to stick to our schedule and disconnect.

Often, the only break we do take is for lunch. And even that "break" is often only the five minutes it takes to grab food and bring it back to our desk.

It turns out the greatest enemy of breaks is most often ourselves and not our managers or organisations.

But breaks are actually quite important for our happiness, our health, our overall well-being, and our performance.

And the great thing is, good quality performance enhancing breaks can take less than a minute.

A day without breaks is for the mind what driving without gas could do to your car. Isn't it true that when you see your deposit low you stop to refuel?

Taking mindful breaks is both a time-efficient and nourishing way of maintaining focus and clarity.

A mindful break is about giving your mind a chance to recover from the constant activity work requires and briefly move from a "doing" state to a "being" state. This state gives our mind a chance to simply be.

It can be just few seconds. Long enough to move from the 'doing' to the 'being' and be aware of your presence.

The benefits of allowing our brains small, regular breaks from conceptual activity are numerous: our brain is re-energized, our mind is more focused and clearer, our body is more relaxed, and we break our action addiction vicious circle.

Obviously, you won't always be able to take a performance break every hour because of your schedule.

While mindful breaks are easy to do, they're just as easy to forget. So, one easy way to remember is to use your smartphone alarms or simply every time your phone rings, try taking a mindful breath before you answer. Or every time you transition between activities from meeting to e-mail, e-mail to car, car to home take a short break.

Find out what works best for you. Remember, every time you practice mindfulness, you create more neural connections, making it easier and easier to find your focus and clarity whenever you need it.

Think that Mindfulness is like your smartphone. You can take it anywhere with you.

***Mindfulness At Work Quick Start -Mindful Breaks***

Take a moment to consider two quick questions:

- How often do you take breaks during a workday?
- What keeps you from taking more breaks?

Once you are aware of the above, think what the best way is to include this short but powerful mindful breaks into your schedule.

Once you decide, below some tips on how to reenergize during a break

Let go of your activities. You don't need to go anywhere special. Close your eyes or keep them open, whichever you prefer.

Direct your full attention to your breath. For three breath cycles do the following:

- Breathe in while noticing your breath; breathe out while relaxing your shoulders, neck, and arms.
- Breathe in while focusing fully on your inhale; breathe out while focusing on the exhale.
- Breathe in while enhancing the clarity of your attention; breathe out while maintaining clarity.
- Let go of the exercise. Return to your work with renewed relaxation, focus, and clarity.

If you really want to perform, you need to refuel.

## WELL-BEING

> Mindfulness is a way of befriending
> ourselves and our experience.
>
> Jon Kabat-Zinn

# Conserve Energy

We are usually aware of our sources of energy, like sleep, nutrition, and physical exercise, but usually we do not think about the mind's own use and maintenance of energy.

### Learn How to Hibernate

Same as animals, imagine if you could conserve your energy and use it when you need it more.

And actually, you can.

Mindfulness practice is actually a bit like hibernation.

The fact is that our minds uses energy. Quite a good amount of energy. Probably you have had one of those days in front of the computer and by the time you finish you are completely exhausted. Your body hasn't used much. It has been your brain.

According to research, without a trained mind our mind wanders almost half of our waking hours. When our minds wander, and we are not focused we are wasting energy. It is also important where our mind goes when it wanders.

Whether we're worried or if we have a positive thought our brain created spirals that could be draining our energy.

All that thinking uses up glucose and oxygen, the fuel for our brain. Our thoughts have an incredibly powerful impact on our mental health and wellbeing. Positive or negative thinking can be mentally and physically exhausting.

With mindfulness practice, you strengthen your focus and awareness giving you the time and ability to choose the objects of your attention, as well as helping you conserve mental energy.

***Mindfulness At Work Quick Start - Mental Energy***

- What are your energy cycles? Morning, afternoon, or evening?

- Look at todays 'task and assign the most challenging ones in the morning, when you have more energy

- Being Present helps you to conserve valuable energy that otherwise would be wasted

- Maintaining Balance in our mind, helps you conserve energy.

- Making Choices: Avoid multitasking and notice the impact that not jumping back and forth between tasks can have on your energy.

> When we get too caught up in the busyness of the world, we lose connection with one another – and ourselves.
>
> Jack Kornfield

## Mindful Exercise

I always feel lazy before going to the gym or doing any type of exercise but the true is that after the session I feel more energized. Can you relate?

We are holistic beings. Your mind and body are connected on a deep level. Energies flow freely between the two. When you have positive physical experiences, your mind smiles.

In this way, caring for the body is just as impactful as caring for the mind. Getting good and sufficient sleep, eating properly, and being physically active are all foundations for both performance and well-being.

Any type of physical activity has a strong positive influence on your body and your brain. Anything that gets you up and moving is a lift to your mind, health, and well-being.

In your everyday work life, take advantage of any opportunity for physical activity. For example, if you are having a call, why don't you walk while talking?

As with mindfulness, there is a tremendous amount of evidence showing the benefits of keeping your body in good shape. This technique examines how mindfulness practice and physical activity make a powerful recipe for better health, increased mental focus, and greater clarity. Let's start by looking at the importance of focus in physical activity.

**Mindfulness At Work Quick Start - Mindful Exercise**

I share with you these 8 tips to include mindfulness in your exercise routine. This proves that you can introduce mindfulness at work. Because Mindfulness doesn't take time. Because mindfulness is about being present. And you are already present. You just need to be aware that you are present. You can be mindful while we are doing other activities. Even while exercising!

1. Pause and consider your purpose. Remember why you want to practice mindfulness. Is it to train your mind to focus and sustain attention? To learn to navigate emotions. Consider your intention for exercise, too. Is it to live longer, lose weight, or have more energy for your kids? This twofold motivation can help get you up and out, and keep you going.

2. Unplug. To meditate during exercise, don't listen to your favourite playlist, talk on the phone, read a magazine, or watch TV. Be fully present where you are: in the woods, on the sidewalk, or on the treadmill.

3. Tap into body sensations. Bring your attention to your physical experience. Are there any parts of your body that are working extra hard? Does your body feel different today than it did yesterday? When I swim, I focus on the

water gliding over my body, the muscles in my arms, and the sensation of my torso rotating with each breath.

4. Use your breath as a cue to challenge yourself more or ease up as necessary. Your inhale or exhale can be an anchor of attention while exercising. If your mind wanders, noticing a new "For Sale" sign in the neighbourhood while you run or recalling an email you forgot to return, just notice the thought, and reconnect with your breath. Observe the tempo of your breath as you work harder and as you cool down.

5. Play with different anchors of attention. Experiment with attentional focal points other than your breath: each full rotation of your bike pedals, the up and down of a lunge. You can switch anchors as you vary your exercise, but stay focused on the rhythm of your anchor, returning to it when your mind wanders.

6. Note your surroundings. There are two aspects of directing attention—focused attention and open awareness—and you can practice both while exercising. To tap into the latter, check out what's around you. How is the air? Temperature? What are you hearing?

7. Renew your resolve — burning hamstrings and all. One of the attitudes of mindfulness is acceptance—not wishing the present moment to be different than it is. Exercising is a brilliant time to practice this. Do you notice any resistance to the workout experience—perhaps wishing you were almost done, or that the pain in your right foot would go away? Commit to your workout time, remember your reasons for being there, and try to stay present from start to finish.

8. Exercise kindness. Notice the quality of your thinking during workouts: Can you appreciate your current ability, speed, and endurance just as they are? If you work out in a group, can you let go of the "comparing mind" and instead thank yourself for showing up for this healthy activity, and then go at the pace that's just right for you?

Any kind of physical activity will help you gain better focus and clarity and by applying the principles of mindfulness you can enhance your performance. By helping you maintain focus, relaxation, and rhythm, mindfulness increases the enjoyment and effectiveness of activity.

> Mindfulness means being awake. It means knowing what you are doing.
>
> Jon Kabat-Zinn

# Eating Mindfully

In the general busyness of everyday, it's easy to default to unhealthy eating patterns.

Like most of us, you've probably eaten something in the past few hours. And, like many of us, you may not be able to recall everything you ate, let alone the sensation of eating it. According to a 2011 report from the U.S. Department of Agriculture, the average American spends two-and-a-half hours a day eating, but more than half the time, we're doing something else, too. Because we're working, driving, reading, watching television, or fiddling with an electronic device, we're not fully aware of what we're eating. And this mindless eating—a lack of awareness of the food we're consuming—may be contributing to the national obesity epidemic and other health issues, says Dr. Lilian Cheung, a nutritionist and lecturer at Harvard T.H. Chan School of Public Health.

While discipline may get you part of the way toward eating well, eating what you like with mindfulness is a gentler and perhaps even more pleasant way to get the energy you need while simultaneously enhancing health and well-being.

To get the most out of mindful eating, there are three basic guidelines: letting your stomach do the eating, avoiding the blood sugar roller coaster, and taking the mindful minute.

### Eat With Your Stomach Not With Your Eyes

Why do we sometimes eat more than we need? Research suggests that when we're too focused on finishing what's in front of us, we lose the mindful awareness that our stomach might already be full. We go on autopilot, eating out of habit rather than necessity.

A simple mindful tip for eating is to let your stomach do the eating. There's no need to finish everything in front of you right this second. When you're full, or even better, before you are full, stop eating. Staying mindfully aware of when you have had enough will not only help you eat better, but feel better too.

But what about those mid-afternoon hankerings for a quick fix of junk food? It turns out, when it comes to sugary snacks, your mind may have a mind of its own.

### The Sugar Crash

Many of us, seeking a quick antidote to feeling sleepy, ride the blood sugar rollercoaster during the afternoon hours. An hour or two after lunch, we hit the afternoon slump a fatigue our brains mistakes for a lack of blood glucose. A natural and automatic reaction is to grab a snack, a cup of coffee, or an energy drink to quickly raise our energy levels. But a snack - and a sugary one in particular -can raise blood sugar levels too high, leading to mood swings, brain fog, and stress.

After a short while, blood sugar levels drop. A sense of panic results due to the stress, cortisol, and adrenaline released when fatigue and brain fog set in. Then we're right back where we started, at the bottom of the roller coaster, with our brains craving another fix of fast energy.

Whether you find yourself at the sugar high or sugar crash, your focus and clarity both suffer. Neither the body nor the brain really needs the extra sugar, no matter how much it might feel like it.

How do we hop off the blood sugar roller coaster? Simple. Take a mindful minute.

**Mindfulness At Work Quick Start - Mindful Eating**

The mindful minute is a self-directed way to avoid undesired and mindless snacking.

With this minute you create the space to mindfully choose what and when you eat.

- Next time you feel desire for food, pause.
- Allow yourself to mindfully observe desire.
- Where do you experience the feeling, in your stomach or elsewhere? Is the experience changing or does it stay the same?
- If after the minute, you're feeling the same desire, you may actually be hungry. In that case, eat.
- If there's little or no desire left, you weren't actually hungry. Your brain tried to trick you. But you were smarter and dismantled the

Mindfulness means focusing on the present moment, while calmly acknowledging and accepting your feelings, thoughts, and bodily sensations. The tenets of mindfulness apply to mindful eating as well, but the concept of mindful eating goes beyond the individual. It also encompasses how what you eat affects the world.

While it's important to stop yourself from eating on autopilot, it's just as important to eat the right amounts of the right foods at the right time and coming from the right places.

The best way to capture moments is to pay attention. This is how we cultivate mindfulness.

Jon Kabat-Zinn

## Enjoying Sleep

Can you think back to a time when you had a good sleep? How did you feel? How did it affect your mood? Your clarity? Your energy?

Now, think about the last time you had a really bad night. Perhaps you were feeling unwell, or your kids, or you just were stress out about a situation at work. How did you feel the following morning?

The long-term effects of sleep deprivation are real.

It drains your mental abilities and puts your physical health at real risk. Science has linked poor slumber with a number of health problems, from weight gain to a weakened immune system.

Many people don't know but while while humans can survive quite a few weeks without food and up to a week without water, they can only go four days without sleep.

Unfortunately, as a result of our busy life, it's often the first thing many of us compromise.

Fortunately, research has shown regular mindfulness practice improves the ability to fall asleep and sleep quality significantly. Whether you are a person who only needs a little sleep or someone who needs a lot, enhancing how quickly and effectively you sleep can enhance performance and make better use of your time.

Equally important to practice mindfulness to enhance your focus and awareness, it is to practice mindfulness to enhance your sleep and waking up.

### Let´s Surf

Melatonin is a hormone the body produces naturally. Natural melatonin is produced primarily by the pineal gland in the brain. Melatonin has a daily bio rhythm—levels rise and fall throughout the day and night, reaching their highest levels in the evening and falling to their lowest levels in the morning. This daily melatonin bio rhythm is strongly tied to the 24-hour cycle of light and dark. This is a key reason why night-time light exposure can be so detrimental to sleep and to health.

It has its own rhythm over a 24-hour period: from very low in the daytime, rising through the evening, and peaking around 2 a.m. By the next morning, melatonin is again down to its low daytime level.

The wave of melatonin it's a lot like surfing: to successfully ride a wave, you need to catch it in its earlier stages. From then on, let it carry you through a good night of sleep, to the shores of morning.

The key to catching the melatonin wave is to be mindful of your own cycle of melatonin and avoid things that can affect your sleep like looking at different digital gadgets right before you go to sleep.

**Turn off screens 60 minutes and relax your late evening activities**

Our cell phones, tablets, computers, and other electronic gadgets have become such a huge part of our daily lives that it's often hard to put them down—even at bedtime. Keeping your phone on your nightstand may not seem like a big deal, but technology affects your sleep in more ways than you realize. Whether you're surfing the web, playing a video game, or using your phone as an alarm clock in the late evening, you're probably keeping yourself from a restful night. Learn the facts about digital devices, below, so you can nip your tech habits in the bud.

**They Suppress Melatonin.**

The blue light emitted by screens on cell phones, computers, tablets, and televisions restrain the production of melatonin, the hormone that controls your sleep/wake cycle or circadian rhythm. Reducing melatonin makes it harder to fall and stay asleep. Most Americans admit to using electronics a few nights a week within an hour before bedtime. But to make sure technology isn't harming your slumber, give yourself at least 60 minutes of gadget-free transition time before hitting the hay. Even better: Make your bedroom a technology-free zone—keep your electronics outside the room (that includes a TV!).

**They Keep Your Brain Alert.**

It may seem harmless to knock out a few emails before bed or unwind with a favourite movie, but by keeping your mind engaged, technology can trick your brain into thinking that it needs to stay awake. And if you're surfing the web, seeing something exciting on Facebook, or reading a negative email, those experiences can make it hard to relax and settle into slumber. After spending an entire day surrounded by technology, your mind needs time to unwind.

**They Wake You Up.**

Just because you're not using your cell phone before bed doesn't mean that it can't harm your sleep: Keeping a mobile within reach can still disturb slumber, thanks to the chimes of late-night texts, emails, calls, or calendar reminders. About 72 percent of children ages six to 17 sleep with at least one electronic device in their bedroom, which leads to getting less sleep on school nights compared with other kids, according to their parents. The difference adds up to almost an hour per night, and the quality of snoozing is negatively affected too. To get a better night's slumber, parents can limit their kids' technology use in the bedroom, and mom and dad should be solid role models and set the tone by doing the same.

Just a small adjustment to your evening routine can go a long way toward enabling you to prepare for bed with a calmer mind that's more in tune with the natural rhythms of your body. So, before going to bed engage with activities that do not require an interaction with devices, or even better, don't do anything at all 30 minutes before going to sleep.

I would have never thought I was going to say this but sometimes procrastination can pay off.

Then, as you let go of the final minutes of the day, consider the following strategies for falling asleep mindfully.

**Your Temple**

The bedroom is our personal space which enables us to relax, revive and refresh, both at the beginning of the day and at the end. Whatever the size of yours, it's vital to ensure it's a haven of tranquillity, peace and calmness. One that will ultimately help you to sleep soundly.

Getting six to eight hours of sleep every night can not only help us to wake up feeling fresh, but it can boost our motivation and energy levels the following day. According to a previous study, the UK's sleep deficit is having a negative impact on our overall productivity, with the average Brit only getting around five hours of shut eye a night.

it's important that your bedroom, the way it is decorated and decluttered, is your sanctuary of peace and rest.

**Waking Up Mindfully**

Robin Sharma says 'the way you begin each day, defines how you'll live each day'

How many of you have had a particularly trying day and thought "I must have woken up on the wrong side of the bed, nothing went right today!"? Perhaps it started with a shaving nick, burnt toast, spilt coffee, missing the bus and being late for work? These are all incredibly luxurious accidents to have I know! Yet this is the world we live in, and these things do genuinely build frustration and anxiety within us. However, chances are they could have been avoided with a little bit of kindness and a good dose of slowing down, to create what I call - a Mindful Morning.

A Mindful Morning does not have to mean an earlier morning (though an extra 10-15 minutes can help!). It means a more present morning to create a mindset of space, calm, and positivity that allows for more effective use of your day.

Researchers have found that many people have the highest level of the stress hormone cortisol in their blood in the minutes after they wake up. This early rush of cortisol is triggered when we immediately start thinking about everything we have to do in the coming day.

Once cortisol has been released into our bloodstreams, our bodies take a long time and a lot of energy to bring the levels back down.

Allowing yourself to wake up peacefully can save you a lot of unnecessarily wasted energy for the rest of the day. Mindfulness can help you minimize or entirely avoid the a.m. cortisol rush.

Even if we don't do it, to wake up mindfully it is easy even if most of the people do not do it.

### Mindfulness At Work Quick Start -Mindful Sleep and Awakening

- Take a moment to reflect on your own sleep patterns.
- Do you get enough sleep at night?
- Are you catching the waves at the right time?
- What types of activities do you do before sleep?
- When you go to bed, are you able to get to sleep quickly?

- What's your experience with the quality of your sleep?
- Is there room for improvement?
- How do you wake up in the morning?

***Sleep***

Now that you are aware of your patters, follow these 9 mindfulness techniques that are related to sleep:

**Beginner's Mind**

- Approach each bedtime with thoughts that are unrelated to past bad nights.
- Do not allow yourself to believe that how you slept last night will influence how you will sleep tonight.
- Do not allow yourself to expect that every night will be a bad night of sleep.
    - Approach the sleep process with no expectations about how your sleep will be.

**Non-striving**

- You can't force yourself to sleep. Falling asleep is NOT a result of effort.
- Think of the process of falling asleep as like digesting food – it just happens.
- Non-striving means striking a balance between your desire for sleep and simply allowing sleep to unfold.

**Letting go**

- Let go of your attachment to the idea that sleep is a problem that needs to be fixed.

- This can also be described as 'letting be' – allow whatever is happening (like not falling asleep) to occur without automatically trying to fix it.
- Avoid labelling yourself as an 'insomniac' and tell others not to ask about how you slept last night.

**Non-judging**

- Don't automatically think of being in bed and awake as negative. This negative energy will work against falling asleep.
- When you are awake in bed tell yourself, you are 'resting' and observe it without judgement.
- Don't think of your sleep as a 'performance' with success or failure.

**Acceptance, or Acknowledgement**

- Choose to accept that you cannot directly control your sleep.
- Efforts to make sleep happen don't generally work.
- Acknowledge that sometimes you will sleep and sometimes you won't.
- This is not the same as 'giving up', which is a value-laden negative concept.

**Trust**

- Trust that your mind and body have the capacity to self-regulate sleep, given the right conditions.
- Be confident that your 'brain isn't broken'.

- Some knowledge about the physical (behavioural) and mental/emotional (cognitive) aspects of good and poor sleep can help you develop this trust (see Understanding and Helping Poor Sleep).

**Patience**

- Results rarely happen immediately so you need to develop patience.
- It is like getting fit at the gym - it takes time.
- Avoid being focussed on the outcome (good sleep) and develop patience in the process itself.

**Gratitude**

- When stressed or sleep deprived it's easy to only think about problems.
- Let your mind redirect its focus away from your sleep and other problems and allow a feeling of gratitude towards some of the good things in your life.

**Generosity**

- Try to give time to friends and colleagues and not be too consumed with your own problems.
- Talking to friends, family and colleagues about their lives can be a meaningful gift to them and a welcome distraction for you and your own worries.

*Awakening*

Tips to wake up mindfully.

**Be prepared**

I might sound like your mother here but - prepare what you need the night before. Have your work bag packed, know what you're taking for lunch, even put clothes out the night before. There is no way you'll be able to add new morning magic to your routine if the basics aren't as quick and easy as they can be.

We've all been there. Trying to get out the door but stuck hopelessly searching for your keys, your phone charger, that document you misplaced. The compound effect of the clock ticking, the hunt that never seems to end, and our "future tripping" over what will happen as a result, induces a state of stress that could so easily have been avoided. This stress can stay with us for the rest of the morning, if not the whole day.

**Behave Mindfully**

Mindfulness does not have to mean meditation. Meditation is simply one form of Mindfulness.

The practice of Mindfulness is by definition "to pay attention, on purpose, without judgement" so if you're not quite ready to give meditating a shot there are plenty of other ways you can behave Mindfully. Slowing the mind makes space for clarity of thought and the freedom to choose how we respond to situations rather than how we react. Without the "what ifs", and the "if only I had done" we train our mind to be truly focused on the here and now. Being present is the aim.

**Embrace Silence**

We as human beings are "always on" - planning the next move, constantly scrolling, checking in, liking, tweeting, emailing. Let me ask you honestly, how many of you now find a moment of idle silence uncomfortable? I challenge you to embrace the silence, even seek it out, once every day. Ideally in the morning.

**Set an intention**

Our thoughts and words yield great power.

Words are incredibly powerful to our mindset, our beliefs, and our sense of self. The more positively we can speak to ourselves, the more positive our experience of the day will be. Starting your day with a positive intention will attract like-for-like in your interactions with others. If you wake up and your first thought is "s**t, I have to deal with that stupid client today. There is no way they are going to understand our requirements, and I'm going to wind up getting nowhere" then you've basically written yourself the script in your first waking breath. Instead try setting yourself the intention "I will creatively seek solutions and am respected and valued regardless of the outcome". Can you see how these words could change your approach to, and experience of the day? An intention becomes your inner compass for the decisions you make - ask yourself "does this choice guide me toward that intention or not?"

Always remember that your day is your life in miniature so how do you live each day is going to have an effect on how you live your entire life.

## THE HOLISTIC YOU

There is not such a thing as work-life balance

You are a holistic being. Whatever you do in any are of your life will have an impact in the rest of the areas.

A holistic approach to your body, mind and soul can not only transform your health and well-being, but it can also benefit your relationships, make your more patient, understanding, loving and generally help you to become more awake as a person in your day-to-day life.

> The essence of bravery is being without self-deception.
>
> Pema Chödrön

# Holistic Approach To Life

Even though I have said I don´t believe in such a thing as work-life balance because we are holistic beings, the true is that many people still refer to it and I think it would be useful to talk about this topic upfront.

While employers can look to studies about what work-life balance means, it's important to remember that work-life balance will always mean something a little different to everyone. Just because an employee fits into a specific generation, this doesn't always mean that they will want the same things as another employee of the same generation. This is where flexibility and workplace happiness come into play.

Before the digital era and the ´always on´ culture, there was a clearer work-home separation. But what the digital era has brought to us is that we are now connected 24/7.

This shift from "work-life separation" to "work-life integration" has happened very quickly. In today's work environments, many people take for granted that they can, and perhaps even should, be connected and available 24–7. But work-life integration, or holistic approach to life, has significant implications for health, happiness, and state of mind.

**Understanding Work-Life Imbalance**

Work-life balance is a state of mind. It is not a physical barrier or line that you can cross. Now even less because of the amount of people working from home.

When people say they're struggling with work-life balance, it means that work is getting in the way of life. It is becoming a problem and it is impacting other areas of life.

The question is, "What can be done?" How can you have a balanced holistic approach to life?

**Moving towards a balanced life**

First of all, it is important to acknowledge that there will be always moments of imbalance.

That is the first step. To be aware that you will always have ups and downs, crisis, and challenging situations.

When you are aware and embrace those difficult moments, you already start building some mental tools to navigate through uncertain times. You are already mentally prepared and that will help manage your fight or flight initial reaction.

**Taking Baby Steps to Manage Work-Life Balance**

Regular mindfulness practice is powerful, so powerful in fact that it rewires your brain, helping you enjoy the good moments in life and build your resilience to imbalance.

You can also try the following tips

**1. Accept that there is no 'perfect' work-life balance**.

When you hear "work-life balance," you probably imagine having an extremely productive day at work and leaving early to spend the other half of the day with friends and family. While this may seem ideal, it is not always possible.

Don't strive for the perfect schedule; strive for a realistic one. Some days, you might focus more on work, while other days you might have more time and energy to pursue your hobbies or spend time with your loved ones. Balance is achieved over time, not each day.

**2. Find a job that you love.**

Although work is an expected societal norm, your career shouldn't be restraining. If you hate what you do, you aren't going to be happy, plain and simple. You don't need to love every aspect of your job, but it needs to be exciting enough that you don't dread getting out of bed every morning.

I recommend finding a job that you are so passionate about you would do it for free. If your job is draining you, and you are finding it difficult to do the things you love outside of work, something is wrong. Hard but plain and simple.

**3. Prioritize your health**

Your overall physical, emotional, and mental health should be your main concern.

Prioritizing your health first and foremost will make you a better employee and person.

**4. Don't be afraid to unplug.**

Cutting ties with the outside world from time to time allows us to recover from weekly stress and gives us space for other thoughts and ideas to emerge. Unplugging can mean something simple like practicing a sport, going for a walk, meditate or just being instead of doing.

**5. Take a vacation.**

Sometimes, truly unplugging means taking vacation time and shutting work completely off for a while. Whether your vacation consists of a one-day staycation or a two-week trip to Bali, it's important to take time off to physically and mentally recharge.

**6. Make time for yourself and your loved ones.**

While your job is important, it shouldn't be your entire life. You were an individual before taking this position, and you should prioritize the activities or hobbies that make you happy. Achieving a balance life requires deliberate action.

If you do not firmly plan for personal time, you will never have time to do other things outside of work. No matter how hectic your schedule might be, you ultimately have control of your time and life.

**7. Set boundaries and work hours.**

Set boundaries for yourself and your colleagues, to avoid burnout. When you leave the office, avoid thinking about upcoming projects or answering company emails. Consider having a separate computer or phone for work, so you can shut it off when you clock out. If that isn't possible, use separate browsers, emails or filters for your work and personal platforms.

Whether you work away from home or at home, it is important to determine when you will work and when you will stop working; otherwise, you might find yourself answering work-related emails late at night, during vacations or on weekends off.

**8. Set goals and priorities (and stick to them).**

Implement time-management strategies, analyse your to-do list, and cut out tasks that have little to no value.

Pay attention to when you are most productive at work and block that time off for your most important work-related activities. Avoid checking your emails and phone every few minutes, as those are major time-wasting tasks that derail your attention and productivity. Structuring your day can increase productivity at work, which can result in more free time to relax outside of work.

Work-life balance will mean different things to different people because, after all, we all have different life commitments. In our always-on world, balance is a very personal thing, and only you can decide the lifestyle that suits you best.

> Nothing ever goes away until it has taught us what we need to know.
>
> Pema Chödrön

## Emotional Balance

Working in any organization can be challenging. Each day, we make choices and act in ways that often have consequences for other people. While sometimes those consequences are positive, that's not always the case. When our actions result in negative consequences for other people, it's normal for them to respond emotionally often in ways that are not helpful for the organization or for their own health and well-being.

Emotions are a natural part of being human. Managed skilfully, they're a powerful source of joy and energy. Unsuccessfully managed, however, they can get in the way, becoming a source of frustration, conflict, and regret.

To be clear, emotional balance has nothing to do with suppressing or getting rid of our emotions. In reality, having emotional balance equates to not getting caught up in the natural ups and downs of our emotions. Emotional balance is a state of being aware of our emotions enough to manage them in a way that is gentle, honest, and wise.

Emotional balance comes from having emotional intelligence combined with a trained mind that's able to notice and respond to emotions when they arise. It makes a significant difference in the work environment in terms of how people interact and work together.

This technique provides some ways to use mindfulness to maintain emotional balance in the midst of emotional turbulence.

**The Basic Reactions to Emotions**

When we face someone joyful, mirror neurons in our brains make us experience a similar joy. The same goes for anger, grief, and almost all other emotions.

Most of us deal with our emotions by either suppressing them or acting them out. The thing about suppressing emotions is that they have to go somewhere. Like pressing down on a balloon. Additionally, suppressing emotions requires an enormous amount of mental energy -energy that's diverted from our own focus and clarity. Acting out our emotions, whether aggressively or passive aggressively, might feel good in the moment. But in the long run, acting out our emotions usually leads to disappointment, regret, or shame.

By utilizing mindfulness, you can maintain emotional balance, even in the face of difficult emotions.

**Maintaining Emotional Balance**

In mindfulness we work to develop the mental capacity, the patience, and the courage to endure discomfort. At the same time, we learn to observe our emotions with some neutrality. We put some kind of distance between our emotions and ourselves. Instead of running on autopilot, we take a moment to pause. We create that space between our automatic reactions, giving ourselves the time, space, and freedom to make conscious, deliberate choices.

To maintain emotional balance, apply these four steps: become aware of the emotion, embrace the emotion, employ patience, and balance, and consciously choose the appropriate response.

### *Mindfulness At Work Quick Start- Emotional Balance*

- The first step, as you can see through this book is awareness
- Take a moment to reflect on how you manage your emotions at work.
- Do you strive to deny and suppress your emotions?
- Or do you act them out?

I leave you with these four steps

### Step #1. Emotional Awareness

In the midst of our everyday busyness, we may default to suppressing our emotions without even consciously realizing we're doing it. We become aware of our emotions when they're strong enough to move to the forefront of our awareness. Therefore, acknowledging the emotion exists is the first step to managing it.

### Step#2. Mindful Embrace

The second is to mindfully embrace the emotion. In other words, simply notice that the emotion is there and hold it without suppressing or acting on it. Being able to see the emotion as an experience, and not letting it overcome you, diminishes its power. Instead of constantly fighting against the emotion, you're able to be with it. When it comes to mindful embrace, your breath can be helpful. While observing the emotion, pay attention to your breath; allow its gentle rhythm to calm you.

### Step#3. Patience and Balance

The third step is to apply patience and balance. Patience is about having the courage to face the discomfort of the emotion.

Whereas patience can help you ride out the emotion, balance can keep you neutral. Balance can help you avoid any automatic aversion or attraction you may have toward it. With the ability to embrace the emotion with patience and balance, you can now maintain the focus and clarity necessary to determine the best, most productive response to it.

### Step#3. Appropriate Response

The fourth and final step involves making a decision choosing the most appropriate response to the situation based on your awareness of the emotion, your embracing of it, and your patience and balance. Of course, the appropriate response is different in each new situation.

Now that you are aware, think about a time when you didn't manage your emotions properly either at work or at home. What would be different today?

> That's life: starting over, one breath at a time.
>
> Sharon Salzberg

# Kindness

If it's true we all want to be happy and no one wants to suffer, what do we need from other people to be happy? Often the answer is simple: things like presence, attention, respect, understanding, and acceptance.

What do other people need from us to be happy?

The exact same things.

### What Does It Mean to Be Kind?

A fundamental pillar of mindfulness isn't too far off from that age-old adage: "May I be happy, and may I do what I can so you can be happy."

However, kindness is not always seen as a priority in the workplace, especially as it can contrast with the traditional image of a successful entrepreneur. Haven't we been told that "nice people finish last?" Office culture can be cutthroat and competitive, leading to hurtful criticism, lack of collaboration, and miscommunication.

However, now we are increasingly talking about wellbeing in the workplace, and bringing an authentic quality to our work, being gentle with ourselves, and with others around us.

A new study in the journal *Emotion* looks at acts of kindness within a real-life working environment and shows how kindness really does create a positive ripple that affects the whole workplace culture. This study has shown that generosity and kindness propagate and spreads. The researchers from the University of California studied workers from Coca Cola's Madrid headquarters. The study group consisted of mostly female employees from a range of departments. Participants were told they were part of a happiness study, and once a week for four weeks, they checked in to report how they were feeling, in terms of mood and life satisfaction, and their experience of positive and negative behaviours. This included how many they had carried out towards others, and how many others had made towards them. Four weeks later, the participants completed further measures, such as happiness and job satisfaction. There was a catch—19 of the participants were instructed by researchers to be the "givers," where each week they performed some act of kindness towards some of their co-workers, who were not part of this control group. It was up to the altruistic group as to what generous acts they performed, and these included relatively simple things that we can often take for granted, such as bringing someone a drink and emailing a thank-you note.

After about a month, the study shows that the acts of kindness don't go unnoticed, and it had a huge impact on the overall positivity in the workplace, and on the employees' sense of wellbeing. The people who received kindness through the 4 weeks reported a sense of camaraderie. In addition, the receivers felt in control at work and reported significantly higher levels of happiness. The acts of kindness, however small and insignificant they might have seemed acted as a buffer even during a period of stress, and difficult work conditions. Even the control group, those 19 people who were part of the control group, enjoyed higher levels of life satisfaction and job satisfaction, and fewer depressive symptoms. They also felt more autonomous, and more competent in their workplace. Therefore, evidence suggests we feel happier when spending money on others than ourselves, and acts of kindness increase not only the receivers but also the giver's sense of wellbeing, autonomy, and competence.

The most interesting aspect of the study was to show that such acts of kindness are also contagious. So, there was an increasing amount of "prosocial" behaviour with employees feeling that they were part of a unit and a workplace that looked after them and cared about them. People not only reciprocated the acts of kindness by taking the initiative to find out who had been kind to them but also paid it forward to others, thereby spreading the feeling of generosity. An additional side-advantage of this was that people were being more creative in how they could show their kindness and generosity, thereby making the employees think outside the box, and exercise creative thinking.

This study, therefore, shows that small acts of kindness not only benefit the receiver, but also the giver and the whole organization, thereby creating a positive workplace culture.

Reality is that even though there are plenty of research, kindness is still considered in some leadership positions as weakness, when in reality is a strength. A strength very closely linked to Emotional Intelligence.

However, many leaders do not allow themselves to be kind. Not only at work, but to themselves.

Think about the airline safety instructions you always hear before take-off: "In case of an emergency, put on your own oxygen mask before assisting others." Why should you help yourself first? Because you can't be of much service to others if you pass out.

In much the same way, the first step in developing kindness is to show kindness to yourself. Give yourself a break. Don't beat yourself up over missteps or mistakes. Instead, treat yourself how you'd like to be treated, with understanding and respect. When you're kind and caring to yourself, it then becomes possible to be truly kind to others.

To increase your capacity for kindness toward yourself and others, incorporate the cultivation of kindness into your daily mindfulness efforts. This includes both in the office with your colleagues and with yourself and loved ones.

**Mindfulness At Work Quick Start - Kindness**

- When you have a difficult situation, talk from you true self and from your caring being and you will notice the difference.

- The more you do it the easier it is going to be thanks to neuroplasticity.

See these random acts of kindness. Small things make a difference.

1. **Buy coffee for everyone on the team**. Pick a random and surprise your colleagues by bringing everyone their favourite drink.

2. **Share fresh baked goods with the office**. When co-workers come into the office, what if there were a selection of donuts and pastries waiting for their arrival?

3. **Pack an extra snack**. Not all acts of kindness need to be grand gestures. You can just share a snack with one colleague on a day she seems out of sorts. Pack an extra one in your lunch or keep a few in your drawer for such an occasion.

4. **Take a colleague out to lunch**. What does a lunch really cost when compared to someone's happiness? For no more than 10 bucks, you could make that person's day — if not the entire week. Do it on a Monday to help ease him back into the workweek.

5. **Extend an invitation**. No matter the workplace, it'll naturally develop circles of friends. If someone often lunches or grabs coffee alone, consider extending an invite to join

6. **Go the extra mile**. Offering to help out a co-worker is one of those acts of kindness that can go over rather well.

7. **Mentor a new colleague**. Think back to your first few months on the job. Chances are, you felt like a fish out

of water. Anyone new to the office probably feels the same. Offer your help to mentor someone.

8. **Share out a little praise**. Not all praise needs to come from leadership to have an impact. But be specific and authentic to make it a real act of kindness.

9. **Put it in words**. There's a reason they say, "It's the little things that mean the most." So, do something small like going by someone's desk to say good morning or good night or thank you for your help.

> The art of peaceful living comes down to living compassionately & wisely.
>
> Allan Lokos

## Cultivate Joy

While feelings such as happiness usually come from external sources and are temporary, joy comes from within and is always abiding. It is an innate part of who you are and how you express yourself. Just watch how babies delight in the simplest things—their emotions are raw and true. It is difficult to feign joy.

What sparks the joy within is unique to you? It could be related to finding a purpose, a calling, or fulfilling a mission. It could be the feeling of being surrounded by family or good friends. Whatever it is that rejuvenates your spirit, do more of that! The reward of living a more fulfilled life is worth the effort that it sometimes takes.

Joy boosts our energy and performance; it enhances our ability to do good work and excel at business. Like all feelings, joy is something we can enable inside ourselves.

Negative states of mind, such as anger or frustration, do not make us feel good physically.

Positive states of mind, such as happiness and joy, do feel good.

Feelings such as anger and joy are not necessarily dependent on what our surroundings throw at us. We can evoke them at will.

Just close our eyes and think about a time you were extremely happy: you baby was born, your wedding, a lunch with friends….

How do you feel?

Now do the opposite. Think close your eyes and think about a time you were sad or stressed. Experience for a moment the energy in your body.

Let's take a look at the impact of joy as opposed to anger on our nervous system.

### Mente Sana in Corpore Sano

The human brain has a tendency to focus on the negative as you take in information; this is known as negativity bias.

And now you know that when we're feeling threatened or stressed, our sympathetic nervous system goes into "fight or flight" mode the same physical mode we'd be in if we were in serious danger. When we're relaxed and at ease, our parasympathetic nervous system puts the body into "rest and digest" mode, and we are more open to enjoying the moment.

Understanding the impact of our mental state on our body is important for enhancing both well-being and performance. Cultivating joy enables us to rebalance our nervous system when we're faced with a perceived threat, giving us that space between responding rashly and responding with clarity and calm. It can also help us sleep better and digest food more effectively.

There may be times where you need to intentionally focus on ways to produce more positive experiences in order to diffuse a bit of that negativity.

**Joy is also contagious.**

Happiness is not something we only enjoy on our own. When you're happy, it has an infectious and measurable effect on the people around you. In other words, not only does joy have a positive impact on your own nervous system but it also helps others feel calm and relaxed.

Consciously or subconsciously, we look to the people around us for cues to how we should behave and feel in any given situation. Scientists have identified what they call "mirror neurons" in the brain that underlie our tendency to copy or reflect what someone else is feeling. It's the reason a laughing baby might cause us to smile or seeing someone we love in pain may cause us to tear up.

Given how easily our behaviour can impact others in our environment, it's worth pausing to think about the ways positive emotions like joy can be beneficial to you, your colleagues, and your organization.

I'm not suggesting it's always easy to be joyful nor should we be hard on ourselves when we feel angry or upset. We all lead busy lives with many demands but fortunately, we can train ourselves to have more joy in our lives. We don't need to wait for it to find us we can proactively choose joy.

If you find yourself doubting this could ever be you, know that you can put practices in place to help and you can do the same in the middle of your busy live. The office is a terrific place to enable joy.

***Mindfulness At Work Quick Start - Cultivating Joy***

Look at Your life and have a gratitude of all positive things you have around you: health, family, house, your eyes, your breath

We give thing for granted but when we have gratitude for the small things in life, we cultivate joy and learn to value them more.

Most of us are "always on," always connected, always running from one thing to the next. The key to cultivating joy is to enjoy your daily activities.

Give yourself the opportunity to let go of your task lists and ambitions. Let go of performing. Just be.

To create joy in the workplace, here are a few things to consider:

**Leadership** - As with any part of a company's culture, the attitude of leadership is key to the success of the program. They must be willing to cultivate joy not just at work, but in their own lives as well. They must "walk the walk" as an example for employees to buy into joy as a part of the culture. The setting must be appealing and comfortable, as well as motivating- everything from the wall colour, artwork and furnishings must be considered.

**Open Up** – In addition to advocating and creating the right infrastructure, leaders should "open up" as well. If others see what makes their boss joyful, they will be more likely to do the same, and that positive influence can be contagious. Photos, mementos, and personal items that connect employees to the things in their life are healthy to have and can open up discussions that lets them talk about things that are important to them and give them joy.

**Personalized Incentives** - Since employees differ from one another, it may also be time to look at the type of incentives given for a job well done. The time of "one size fits all" may need to be retired and rewards based on the individual and what motivates them take the forefront of any recognition program. By personalizing the incentive, the manager and the company is telling the employee that it knows them as an individual and that they have different needs and desires than other employees.

**Avoid Burnout** - Employee burnout is a morale killer, and managers must constantly be on the lookout. To help avoid burnout as an issue, leadership needs to be comfortable in demonstrating and promoting emotional skills that nurture joy, empathy, generosity, and humility.

**Tailor Recognition** - It is important to note that while recognition is a great thing for employee morale, it may be best to keep it to a private conversation between the manager and the employee. While publicly announcing a big "way to go" in front of peers sounds like a great idea, a slippery slope may be created if someone else involved in the project was unintentionally overlooked and doesn't get the same recognition by the boss.

**Building the Right Team** - But what happens when someone isn't a "fit" or is a negative influence and is causing the joy to leave the office? This is bound to happen on occasion as not everyone is going to be the perfect person for the job or fit for the company. Sometimes an employee can turn it around and bounce back, but not always. When this does happen, it will need to be dealt with as quickly as possible while leaving the person's dignity and honour intact. Nothing is a greater morale buster than an employee that has a cloud of negativity following them around and affecting others.

**Hiring for Joy** - On the front end, it is better to take the time to hire the right person for the job and to look for someone who wants to help cultivate joy and expects it as part of the job description. There is a saying that goes along the lines of "employees don't leave companies, companies leave people".

# INTRODUCING MINDFULNESS IN THE WORKPLACE

> Whether you think you can or you can't you're right
>
> Henry Ford

## Introducing Mindfulness In The Workplace

Before you can even get your organisation or employees to buy into the idea of Mindfulness At Work, you will need to be mindful yourself and work with other leaders to practice and implement the same behaviours.

### Developing Mindful Leaders

Often leaders are focused on actions, tasks, and results. Mindful leaders are present and attentive to the needs of the organization. They focus on what's going well, what teams need to get their jobs done, listening, and asking questions. By being mindful, they in turn encourage diversity and inclusion, bolster creativity, and develop buy-in to the mission from employees.

By teaching leaders to be more mindful, they can shift to a mindset of focus and awareness of both themselves and the business. Being able to engage in self-reflection and greater empathy is going to bear the best results – knowing how a situation makes someone feel and how to best respond.

This is an important part of what it means to develop emotional intelligence (EQ). Understanding and managing emotions can help relieve stress, boost communication, help develop empathy, and resolve conflict.

Here some tips for the leader within you:

**1. Lead By Example**

Asking of others what you don't yet have yourself only promotes inauthentic behaviour. First, be what you ask others to become. A lack of mindfulness in your organization, division or team is a direct expression of your own lack of value clarity. Mindfulness does not demand or desire. Mindfulness allows, and through its acceptance, it attracts others to value and practice.

**2. Give People Time To Dream**

Leaders don't need to control every minute of their employees' days. It makes it hard for employees to use their imagination as we have seen in the mindful creativity chapter.

**3. Look At Your Response From Another's Point of View**

When in doubt, don't send the email, make the call or start a meeting until you feel clear, calm and confident. There's nothing worse than responding with attitude and paying the price later with self-doubt or anxiety. Always think of your actions from another's point of view and take their perspective into consideration. This action alone can go a long way toward creating a mindful workplace.

## 4. Ask Challenging Questions

Great leaders ask great questions. The leader who wants to inspire their team to think bigger should ask questions to challenge the thinking of their team. Questions call people to act and think. Each week, a leader can ask their team a question about how to improve the company and the organization, and watch the ideas, suggestions and comments lead to productivity, engagement, and breakthroughs.

## 5. Get Up And Take A Break

Let your team see you take breaks. Get out from under the work pile. It's hard but necessary to ensure best efforts are put forth. Taking a physical break, getting up from the computer and walking away, forces the mind back to present. The shift in both mental and physical activity creates a space for rest and rejuvenation. With a refreshed mind and body come new ideas and renewed commitment.

## 6. Teach People How To Practice Mindfulness

Teach people what mindfulness is and help them experience it for themselves. Giving people some simple mindfulness tools can help them become more aware of how they feel and react to emotion, more observant of their inner and outer worlds and more present in how they listen and communicate, raising the overall level of consciousness in the workplace.

## 7. Remember To Breathe

People react out of urgency in our disruptive world and throw words out of their mouths every second. Overstimulated people with big egos think innovation is more important than human kindness. People need to stop talking and start breathing. Breathe as you sit in your conference room, think about the lives before you and speak mindfully with human-centred intention.

### 8. Notice The Little Things Around You

Even a few minutes throughout your day can make a difference. Notice the small things around you. Your colleagues, your job, your office…and have gratitude for things you have. Even if small.

### 9. Lead With Emotional Connection

You have to be emotionally present, especially when people are facing the dragon. To really understand the emotional reality for people and their struggles and create an emotional alliance in order to help them overcome the challenges, address their emotional blocks and reconnect the team together. Without this, people will not perform to the best of their abilities.

### 10. Allow Gap Time Between Meetings

Most workplaces have back-to-back meetings, where people race from one meeting to the next without a moment to breathe or think. Employees are either late to the next meeting or check out of their prior meeting early, mentally, or physically. This is true for virtual meetings, as well. Allowing five to 10 minutes between meetings increases focus, productivity, and well-being for everyone.

## 11. Slow Down And Block 'Unscheduled' Time For Yourself

The best thing you can do to encourage mindfulness is slow down. Speed has a way of perpetuating itself and, unfortunately, can trigger the fight or flight response. Slow down; check in with your body and breath. Purposefully blocking unscheduled time and getting out of your normal routine can also help to increase mindfulness.

## 12. Don't Be A Micromanager

Yoga and massage therapists at work are positive, but if you want more mindfulness among team members, start by giving people space and time to be mindful. Stress is a major block to mindfulness, and one of the biggest stressors is -- you guessed it -- micromanagement. So, remember, it's not necessary to hover, and doing so not only affects morale; it prohibits free thinking and creativity.

## 13. Incorporate Mindfulness Into Meetings

One of the things that I recommend, as seen in mindful meetings, is to take a few minutes at the beginning of a meeting to meditate, set intentions and take a few breaths. I have found that this allows for mindfulness to be an action item and incorporated into the culture of the organization, as it shows the importance of it in all aspects of life. -

## 14. Start A Conversation About Mindfulness

Mindfulness can be frightening to the uninformed. People often do not realize that mindfulness can be accessed through a multitude of approaches. Starting a conversation where other team members reveal the techniques that work for them can help people struggling with the concept understand and de-mystify the topic

Talking of which, let's see how you can introduce Mindfulness at your organisation.

### *Introducing Mindfulness in your organisation*

Up to this point we have focused on you and how mindfulness at work can help you enhance your focus, achieve more (doing less!), and improve your well-being

If you want to introduce mindfulness into the organisation, there are few things to take into account to be successful:

### 1. Get Leaders on board.

If your leadership team is not willing to explore or even try mindfulness in the workplace, then your efforts will be for nothing.

We have talked about the benefits of mindfulness, so you could think that it is a no brainer. However, you need to speak their language.

The word mindfulness itself can raise concerns about something spiritual or taking time out. And you know that is not the case.

It is important to provide clear and effective communication about the program.

- What is mindfulness
- Whom it´s for
- Explain the benefits

Consider changing the name and not using mindfulness at all. You know your organisation. Figure out what terminology best fits your organisation´s culture and objectives.

**2. Company Goals.**

Another way of easily convincing senior leadership is linking mindfulness to your company goals.

You know the benefits. Mindfulness means focus, attention, creativity and productivity among many other benefits directly linked to the company success and the well-being of the employees.

You can explain the business benefits of mindfulness- not only the well-being of the employees (that should suffice!) but that it will result in fewer sick days and increased productivity, meaning lower cost and higher revenue.

Now you are talking their language!

 If your office culture is already set up for these practices, then it will be much easier to start. If it isn't, feel out their willingness to explore before you start this process.

**3. Lead by example**

Once you have the company onboard, leaders need to have the commitment to lead by example following some of the tips I shared above.

When you build leadership support, you link the initiative to the company, teams, and individual´s goals, and you communicate appropriately you are setting up for success.

Be the change you want to see in the world

Gandhi

## Life Is A Story; Make Yours The Best Seller

We are getting to the end of our time together and I truly hope that what you have read has helped you to reconfirm (you knew it already) that you are the owner of your thoughts, your actions, and your future.

You are a holistic being and whatever you do in one area of your life is going to have an effect in the other areas.

We all have many projects in our lives: building a great career, having a strong family, being in good physical shape. However, mindfulness practice is not just another project in the procession of these life projects.

It is a way of being. Of being mindful. Of writing Your Best Seller.

Thank you for your presence.

# ANNEX

> The present moment is the only time over which we have dominion.
>
> Thích Nhất Hạnh

## Eight-week Mindfulness At Work Programme

I have shared with you Mindfulness Quick Start tips at the end of each chapter because I strongly believe that when you see the benefits straight away, that builds momentum. That motivation is going give you that action addiction that you are already familiar with. Hopefully, you will see the benefits in your life, and you would like to get more of it.

If that is the case, I have created a downloadable program that will accompany you through this journey.

Mindfulness is not just a theory. Mindfulness is training. And as with any training, you won't achieve results without putting things into practice.

In my Mindfulness At Work Program I integrate elements one step at a time, so it is easy to introduce small habits into your life.

Should you accept the challenge, you can download the program here: https://bit.ly/MINDFULNESSPROGRAM

Your Breath Is Your Brain´s Remote Control

Nieves

# Breathing

A study has found evidence to show that there is actually a direct link between nasal breathing and our cognitive functions.

These findings show a system where our in-breath is like a remote control for our brains: by breathing in through our nose we are directly affecting the electrical signals in the "smell" regions, which indirectly controls the electrical signals of our memory and emotional brain centres. In this way, we can control and optimize brain function using our in-breath, to have faster, more accurate emotional discrimination and recognition, as well as gain better memory.

So, taking a breath in through our nose can control our brain signals and lead to improved emotional and memory processing, but what about the out-breath? As mentioned earlier, slow, steady breathing activates the calming part of our nervous system, and slows our heart rate, reducing feelings of anxiety and stress. So, while the in-breath specifically alters our cognition, the act of slow, deep breathing, whether the inhalation or exhalation, is beneficial for our nervous system when we wish to be more still

### So, let's learn to breath

How do you cultivate mindfulness? One way is to meditate. A basic method is to focus your attention on your own breathing—a practice simply called "mindful breathing." After setting aside time to practice mindful breathing, you'll find it easier to focus attention on your breath in your daily life—an important skill to help you deal with stress, anxiety, and negative emotions, cool yourself down when your temper flares, and sharpen your ability to concentrate.

Time required:

15 minutes daily for at least a week (though evidence suggests that mindfulness increases the more you practice it).

### How to do it:

The most basic way to do mindful breathing is simply to focus your attention on your breath, the inhale and exhale. You can do this while standing, but ideally, you'll be sitting or even lying in a comfortable position. Your eyes may be open or closed, but you may find it easier to maintain your focus if you close your eyes. It can help to set aside a designated time for this exercise, but it can also help to practice it when you're feeling particularly stressed or anxious. Experts believe a regular practice of mindful breathing can make it easier to do it in difficult situations.

Sometimes, especially when trying to calm yourself in a stressful moment, it might help to start by taking an exaggerated breath: a deep inhale through your nostrils (3 seconds), hold your breath (2 seconds), and a long exhale through your mouth (4 seconds). Otherwise, simply observe each breath without trying to adjust it; it may help to focus on the rise and fall of your chest or the sensation through your nostrils. As you do so, you may find that your mind wanders, distracted by thoughts or bodily sensations. That's okay. Just notice that this is happening and gently bring your attention back to your breath.

Find a relaxed, comfortable position. You could be seated on a chair or on the floor on a cushion. Keep your back upright, but not too tight. Hands resting wherever they're comfortable. Tongue on the roof of your mouth or wherever it's comfortable.

Notice and relax your body. Try to notice the shape of your body, its weight. Let yourself relax and become curious about your body seated here—the sensations it experiences, the touch, the connection with the floor or the chair. Relax any areas of tightness or tension. Just breathe.

Tune into your breath. Feel the natural flow of breath—in, out. You don't need to do anything to your breath. Not long, not short, just natural. Notice where you feel your breath in your body. It might be in your abdomen. It may be in your chest or throat or in your nostrils. See if you can feel the sensations of breath, one breath at a time. When one breath ends, the next breath begins.

Be kind to your wandering mind. Now as you do this, you might notice that your mind may start to wander. You may start thinking about other things. If this happens, it is not a problem. It's very natural. Just notice that your mind has wandered. You can say "thinking" or "wandering" in your head softly. And then gently redirect your attention right back to the breathing.

Stay here for five to seven minutes. Notice your breath, in silence. From time to time, you'll get lost in thought, then return to your breath.

Check in before you check out. After a few minutes, once again notice your body, your whole body, seated here. Let yourself relax even more deeply and then offer yourself some appreciation for doing this practice today.

# SERVICES AVAILABLE

## Tools

Download the Mindfulness At Work Program, free of charge at https://bit.ly/MINDFULNESSPROGRAM

Download ScrewProcrastinationTakeAction tools, free of charge, at https://bit.ly/SCREWPROCRASTINATIONTOOLS

## Other Titles

ScrewProcrastinationTakeAction

https://bit.ly/AUTHORNIEVES

## Coaching and Mentoring

You can also read about Life and Corporate and Executive Coaching sessions at **www.fastracktorefocus.com**

## Workshops and lectures

Book Nieves to speak at your event and she's guaranteed to deliver an incredibly inspiring, highly entertaining, and truly life-changing experience for everyone in attendance.

For more information visit www.fastracktorefocus.com

En Español

*https://fastracktorefocus.com/el-club/*

# SOCIAL NETWORKING

Connect with me and join our communities to maintain momentum and connect with positive Accountability Partners

*https://www.linkedin.com/in/managementcoachingconsulting/*

**Facebook**
@Fastrackrefocus

*http://bit.ly/TuFuturoYoFacebook*

**Twitter**
*@fastrackrefocus*

**Instagram**
*Fastracktorefocus Coaching*

**You Tube Fastracktorefocus**

Spotify Tu Futuro Yo Empieza Hoy

Apple Podcast Tu Futuro Yo Empieza Hoy

## ABOUT THE AUTHOR

Nieves Rodríguez is a Business Leader with over 30 years 'experience leading multinational companies. Nieves is a Corporate and Executive Coach, NLP Practitioner and Mindfulness Master and combines her leadership experience with her knowledge to help individuals and businesses to be successful.

She is the founder of FastrackToRefocus Coaching, which vision is helping people and businesses connect with their true values and whys to achieve their goals both personally and professionally.

Nieves has over 25 years' experience leading multinational companies in different parts of the globe. She is an inspirational leader with excellent track record leading teams, launching start-ups, turn around projects and, in a nutshell, making things happen. A highly committed Leader and Life, Corporate & Executive qualified Coach with a strong focus on execution of strategy while capable of engaging individuals and leading teams.

During her career, she has learned the importance of having a people-centred leadership and drive. This is what her business offers to individuals and organizations. She is very much a performance and results-oriented coach and uses her life and corporate experience to work closely with her clients.

**Nieves believes in a holistic approach, to be leaders in all aspects of our life, not just in our careers**

Her life is full of examples of her philosophy in practice on a personal and professional level.

**This is her mission in life now: To empower people and businesses to achieve their full potential.**

Nieves loves travelling, meditating, reading, drinking coffee and enjoys good chats with her friends and family!!

For more information on Nieves' Coaching Business, Workshops, Keynote Speaking and books, visit http://www.fastracktorefocus.com

**AUTHOR PAGE AND OTHER BOOKS AVAILABLE AT AMAZON**

https://bit.ly/AUTHORNIEVES

**ABOUT**

https://www.linkedin.com/in/managementcoachingconsulting/

Printed in Great Britain
by Amazon